Launch the Lifeboat to Read and Spell

Book 4

Lifeboat
Book 4

First edition published by The Robinswood Press 2000

© Jacqueline Davison, Michael Davison,
Sula Ellis and Tony Ellis 2000

Sula Ellis, Tony Ellis, Jacqueline Davison and Michael Davison
have asserted their rights under the Copyright, Designs and
Patents Act 1988 to be identified as the authors of this work.

Design and illustrations:
© Stephen Emms, Phil Goundrey, Henry Marshall and
The Robinswood Press 2000.

This version (v1.4) printed by Blueprint Design & Graphics Limited.

The Robinswood Press

Malvern   England
www.robinswoodpress.com

ISBN 1-869981-650

Contents

About the Authors

Sula Ellis   BA (Hons)   PGCE (Distinction)   DipSpLD (Dyslexia Institute)   AMBDA
Tony Ellis MBA BEng DipSpLD (Hornsby International Dyslexia Centre)

Sula and Tony Ellis of *Ellis Dyslexia Consultants* have many years' combined experience as Special Needs teachers, running units in Berkshire and Surrey in addition to tutoring in both the state and private sectors. Sula Ellis has taught as an OCR lecturer at East Berkshire College, training teachers to Diploma level in Special Needs. She is completing doctoral research in Dyslexia and Mathematics with Professor TR Miles, University of Wales, Bangor and Professor TJ Wheeler, Principal of University College, Chester.

Jackie Davison BTech (Hons) DipSpLD (Hornsby International Dyslexia Centre)
Mick Davison DipSpLD (Hornsby International Dyslexia Centre)

Jackie and Mick Davison are based in Hertfordshire where they provide a successful Learning Support service through *Davison Dyslexia Tutors.* They are directly involved in specialist teaching for a large number of pupils, generally in the age range of 7 to 13 years.

Acknowledgements

The production of a work of this magnitude required considerable support from colleagues and other professionals in the area of Special Needs who provided encouragement, advice, expertise and appraisal.

The authors would particularly like to thank teachers from the two hundred Berkshire schools who took part in the original MBA research project, which led to the development of the Lifeboat scheme, by completing questionnaires and providing practical guidance on their needs; Jan Donlon for the extensive typing task; Matthew Turner for suggesting the title; and all the many students who, during the trial period of *Lifeboat,* have given us such constructive feedback.

The title – *Launch the Lifeboat to Read and Spell* – derives from the ex-RNLI Watson Class lifeboat which, after helping to save 160 lives while in service at Southend-on-Sea and Beaumaris, became the authors' headquarters for the development and realisation of this scheme. It deserved its own special acknowledgement.

Foreword

It gives me great pleasure to commend this Resource Pack. I know it to be based on the authors' many years' experience in the teaching of dyslexic children and on their knowledge of what these children are likely to find difficult. Moreover, this Pack so obviously represents 'good practice' that one can recommend it as being suitable for teaching reading and spelling to *all* children, whether dyslexic or not. I have never seen dyslexic children as a 'race apart': as I see the situation, it is simply that non-dyslexic children pick many things up for themselves which dyslexic children need to have carefully explained to them.

This is how the authors themselves describe the programme: *"the lesson topics are highly structured to present spelling rules, specific letter blends and phonics in a multi-sensory way"*. There is, in fact, wide agreement among teachers in the English-speaking world that a programme of this kind is the most appropriate and effective one for dyslexic individuals of all ages who are struggling to become literate. The present Resource Pack is innovative, however, in that it allows class teachers to teach the class as a whole in advance of the time when the children will be working at their own workbooks. This seems to me highly cost effective use of teachers' time: it combines the social advantages of group work with the opportunity for children to have their own individualised programmes and progress at their own speed.

To all who use the Resource Pack, teachers and students alike, I send my good wishes.

Professor TR Miles MA PhD CPsychol FBPsS

Now that all children are expected to be included in the mainstream classroom, it is most appropriate that this resource pack has been made available, based on the principles espoused by the founders of the 'multi-sensory' approach to teaching SpLD and dyslexic students. With this scheme, the 20 per cent who have always found difficulty with reading, writing, spelling – and sometimes mathematics - will have an opportunity to learn more easily. It is only by targeting the 20 per cent that true literacy across the range of those at risk can ever be achieved. Of course, those with severe problems will probably still need extra help, but at least this will be in line with that being taught in the classroom rather than in conflict with traditional teaching.

In addition, this scheme is applicable to all age groups from primary through secondary into tertiary and adult dyslexic units. It therefore not only makes integration possible – it also benefits those without any learning difficulties by teaching them grammar, punctuation and sentence construction.

Professor Bevé Hornsby
MBE PhD MSc MEd FRCSLT AFBPsS HonFCP FRSA AMBDA

Introduction

The Lifeboat Scheme – Structured, Comprehensive and Cumulative

The Lifeboat scheme was designed to help develop the reading and spelling skills of *all* students. Great care was taken in its development to meet the requirements of the general classroom, especially for independent and differentiated work, and the need for a precise, step-by-step, accumulative approach for students identified as requiring specialist tuition in order to grasp the essentials of the English language.

The Lifeboat scheme meets these requirements by being entirely self-contained and by having a highly structured, comprehensive programme, presented in a standard format of multi-sensory exercises. This particular book is one of ten, each of which contain ten lessons, with each lesson consisting of eight A4 worksheets. The scheme is described in detail in the Introduction to Book 1 and on the publisher's web site (www.robinswood.co.uk). The Lesson Format (see Book 1 or www) provides details on the aims and use of each worksheet. The Programme Structure is an important reference source for users and has been included in all ten books. It is designed for use as a wall chart for cross-reference to all scheme lessons.

Lifeboat lessons progress in a sequential, step-by-step manner to develop a deeper understanding of phonics used in the English language. Each lesson covers just one topic, and incorporates only those phonics, letters and blends which have been covered in previous lessons. This gives the student the opportunity to build cumulatively on earlier groundwork and establishes the potential for continual achievement and 'success' for the student. Topics on vowels, digraphs, blends, diphthongs, prefixes, suffixes and syllables are thus presented in a structure that carefully builds from the very early stages to more demanding concepts.

Since the programme can be used by all school children, and since the actual layout enables each student to work independently, the scheme can be used *differentially* by the whole class in a group setting. It is therefore invaluable for work during The Literacy Hour, especially since it includes exercises which improve skills at word, sentence and text levels. Once pupils have become familiar with the worksheet format they may also work on the lessons unsupervised, whether at school or at home. The lessons can therefore be used for independent study, holiday work and reading homework.

Multi-sensory Approach

The format of the Lifeboat worksheets and the approach used in individual exercises draws on the principles of *multi-sensory* teaching methods recommended, for example, by the British Dyslexia Association. It is felt that the most successful way to help students with literacy difficulties at any level is with exercises requiring *visual, kinaesthetic* and *auditory* sensory channels. 'Speaking' aloud, becoming 'involved' with a particular sound, as well as simply 'looking' at letters and words on the page all help the student to gain knowledge and command.

The result of this approach is that students are much more likely to learn effective strategies with which to overcome their areas of difficulty and which assist them to recall information from memory more efficiently. As a consequence, the individual student may come to access the richness of the English language with far greater depth and with a more satisfying sense of achievement.

'User-friendly' Format

The structure of the programme and the format of the individual lessons have been designed with the need for independent working in mind. The format of the worksheets remains consistent, after a few introductory lessons in Book 1, and this contributes to the ease with which students can work on their own. Although it is always valuable to have recourse to trained specialist staff, the scheme is straightforward to operate and the student's progress can be readily monitored with the materials supplied. It can therefore be managed very successfully not only by the specialist, but also by the classroom teacher, the classroom assistant and by parents themselves.

The user is referred to as 'student' throughout, since those who will benefit from the scheme are in a wide age range: from primary school children to secondary, further and higher education students, adult learners, those with English as a second language, etc. The exercises have been designed to appeal across this range.

Using the Lifeboat Scheme

The reader is strongly recommended to study the Teaching Guide provided in full in the Introduction to Book 1 and on www.robinswood.co.uk. This provides an overview of the structure of the scheme, the *Skill Aims* and *Golden Teaching Tips.*

Assessment sheets, with detailed explanation, are also provided to help identify the point on the programme that would be most appropriate to a particular student or class. In addition, Book 1 includes a Record Chart, a Student Progress Chart and a Student Certificate Achievement.

Since most users of this scheme will have the full set of Lifeboat books, or at least the early books in the series, and since most educational establishments and many parents have ready access to the internet, it seemed wasteful of both forest and financial resources to reprint these extra ten pages in Lifeboat Book 2 to 10. It is hoped that users of the scheme will not feel inconvenienced. However, users are welcome to contact the publisher if they have any difficulty in accessing the detailed introduction.

Lifeboat
Programme Structure

Book 1   *Lesson 1*   **Alphabet Sequencing**
  Lesson 2   **Consonants**
  Lesson 3   **Vowels**
  Lesson 4   **i**
  Lesson 5   **i n p s t**
  Lesson 6   **a**
  Lesson 7   **b d**
  Lesson 8   **sn sp st**
  Lesson 9   **-nd -nt**
  Lesson 10   **Review and Post-test**

Book 2   *Lesson 1*   **e**
  Lesson 2   **Open and Closed Syllables**
  Lesson 3   **k**
  Lesson 4   **Compound Words**
  Lesson 5   **v̆c / cv Syllable Breakdown**
  Lesson 6   **One Syllable Two Syllables**
  Lesson 7   **o and u**
  Lesson 8   **-ck**
  Lesson 9   **br cr dr fr gr pr tr**
  Lesson 10   **Review and Post-test**

Book 3   *Lesson 1*   **-ick -ic**
  Lesson 2   **scr spr str**
  Lesson 3   **i-e**
  Lesson 4   **bl cl fl gl pl sl spl**
  Lesson 5   **al -all**
  Lesson 6   **Vowel -y**
  Lesson 7   **-ff -ll -ss**
  Lesson 8   **Suffixes -est -less -ly -ness**
  Lesson 9   **Syllable Division v̆c / cv v̄ / cv**
  Lesson 10   **Review and Post-test**

Book 4   *Lesson 1*   **a-e**
  Lesson 2   **e-e**
  Lesson 3   **fl fr gl gr**
  Lesson 4   **o-e**
  Lesson 5   **-ng -nk -ing**
  Lesson 6   **-are -ire -ore**
  Lesson 7   **u-e**
  Lesson 8   **sc sk sm sw**
  Lesson 9   **-lb -lf -lk -lt -mp -ct -ft -xt**
  Lesson 10   **Review and Post-test**

This chart shows the detailed structure of the Lifeboat programme.

The student undertaking the complete programme progresses sequentially through Lessons 1 to 10 in each of the Books 1 to 8. This provides a cumulative, comprehensive knowledge of the essential constituents of the English language.

The lessons in Books 9 and 10 act as a supplement to the main programme. They are particularly suitable for work with the class or group as a whole.

When used with the main programme of Books 1 to 8, the lessons in Books 9 and 10 should ideally be integrated with those of Books 4 to 7 at the points which are indicated in the chart.

Book 10, Lesson 10 is the final Review for the complete Lifeboat scheme.

Book 9

Doubling Letters   *Lesson 1*
Magic 'e' Vowel Review   *Lesson 2*
-zz -ze -se -s (z) Sound   *Lesson 3*
'H' Brothers ch sh th   *Lesson 4*
Days and Months   *Lesson 5*
Numbers   *Lesson 6*
Contractions   *Lesson 7*
Plural -es   *Lesson 8*
Suffix Drop 'e'   *Lesson 9*
Prefixes   *Lesson 10*

Book 10

Lesson 1 **Suffix Drop 'y'**

qu squ -que	*Lesson 1* **Book 5**
ee oo	*Lesson 2*
ar er or	*Lesson 3*
-ed	*Lesson 4*
-ay	*Lesson 5*
-ce -se -nce	*Lesson 6*
Soft 'c' (s) Sound	*Lesson 7*
-ge -dge -age	*Lesson 8*

Lesson 2 **Soft 'g' (j) Sound**

ch -tch	*Lesson 9*
Review and Post-test	*Lesson 10*

-ble -dle -gle -ple -tle -zle	*Lesson 1* **Book 6**
ea ee	*Lesson 2*
ai -ain	*Lesson 3*
ir	*Lesson 4*
oa	*Lesson 5*

Lesson 3 **ou (ow) Sound**

-ow	*Lesson 6*

Lesson 4 **Silent Letters**

Lesson 5 **Change f /fe to -ves**

igh	*Lesson 7*

Lesson 6 **ur**

au -aw	*Lesson 8*

Lesson 7 **-ew**

-tion	*Lesson 9*
Review and Post-test	*Lesson 10*

Lesson 8 **ie**

Odd Plurals Plural Review	*Lesson 1* **Book 7**
Wild Old Words	*Lesson 2*

Lesson 9 **ei**

ph -gh (f) Sound	*Lesson 3*
oi -oy	*Lesson 4*
ear	*Lesson 5*
wh 'H' Brothers Review	*Lesson 6*
Schwa	*Lesson 7*
ch (3 Sounds)	*Lesson 8*
-an -en -ant -ent -ancy -ency	*Lesson 9*
Review and Post-test	*Lesson 10*

ou (7 Sounds)	*Lesson 1* **Book 8**
-ey	*Lesson 2*
-ure -ture	*Lesson 3*
-al -el	*Lesson 4*
-us -ous -ious	*Lesson 5*
-sion	*Lesson 6*
-ar -or (er) Sound	*Lesson 7*
-cian	*Lesson 8*
ci si ti xi	*Lesson 9*
Review and Post-test	*Lesson 10*

Lesson 10 **Review of Whole Scheme**

Lesson Notes to Book 4

Lesson 1 **a-e**

The exercises in this lesson build on the early work carried out and the knowledge concerning **i-e** which was gained in Book 3, Lesson 3. [*Sight word*: 'USA'. *Early words*: 'pla_y_', 'f_i_nd'.]

Lesson 2 **e-e**

With this lesson, the three combinations **a-e e-e** and **i-e** are completed. Watch out for **-ere** making the sound (ear) as in 'here'. [*Sight word*: 'their'. *Early words*: '_C_hinese', 'a_th_lete', '_s_wede', '_e_lect', '_th_eme', 'ev_en_', 'in_t_erfere', '_c_ompete', '_c_omplete', '_c_ompare', '_th_ese', 'Stev_en_', 'a_dd_', 't_oo_', 'ra_ce_', '_Ch_ristmas', 'gi_ft_s', 'comm_on_', 'e_x_treme'.]

Lesson 3 **fl fr gl gr**

Book 2, Lesson 9 introduced **r** blends, and **l** blends were featured in Book 3, Lesson 4. The four blends **fl fr gl gr** are presented in this lesson in the context of other letter combinations which have been introduced since the four blends here were worked upon initially.

Lesson 4 **o-e**

This lesson extends the range of magic **'e'** coverage to four combinations: **a-e e-e i-e** and **o-e**. Such words as 'globe' can now be included. The student is faced with a greater challenge in this topic when a consonant blend is included at the start of the word, both for reading and for spelling. [*Early words*: 'st_ore_', 'a_tt_ic', 'ro_se_', 'no_se_', '_s_cone', 'po_se_', '_b_eh_i_nd', 'clo_se_'.]

Lesson 5 **-ng -nk -ing**

The letters **-ng -nk** in this lesson usually come on the end of one-syllable words straight after a short vowel. The sound of the **n** is made in the throat. The suffix **-ing** adds to the knowledge introduced in Book 3.

Lesson 6 **-are -ire -ore**

These exercises deal with the letter **r** which is 'rotten' - it spoils the sound of vowels around it. The sounds in the combinations **a-e i-e o-e** are changed because of the **r** in the middle, for example, in the words 'stare', 'fire' or 'snore'. [*Sight words*: 'what', 'have', 'some'. *Early words*: '_s_care', '_s_core', '_th_an', '_o_ld', 'ni_l_'.]

Lesson 7 **u-e**

This lesson draws on the experience gained from the other magic **'e'** lessons: **a-e e-e i-e o-e** and now **u-e**. Exercises recognise that this combination also produces two sounds, (o͞o) as, for example, in 'Luke', and (ū), for example, as in 'tune'. [*Sight word*: 'London', 'T.V'. *Early words*: '_u_se', 'a_mu_se', 'in_f_late', '_a_buse', '_a_ccuse', '_a_cute'.]

Lesson 8 **sc sk sm sw**

The blends **sn sp** and **st** were introduced in Book 1, Lesson 8. Blends **scr spr** and **str** featured in Book 3, Lesson 2, and **sl** and **spl** appeared in Book 3, Lesson 4. This lesson now features the remaining **s** blends of **sc sk sm** and **sw**. Remember, from Book 2, Lesson 3, that **k** likes to be followed by **i e** and **y**. This knowledge is helpful for choosing between **sc** and **sk**. Note how the 't' has changed in the word 'Scotland'. [Early word: 'Ma_c_'.]

Lesson 9   **-lb -lf -lk -lt -mp -ct -ft -xt**

This lesson features quite a number of end blends such as **-lb -lf -lk -lt -mp -ct -ft -xt** in which each constituent consonant sound can be heard. [*Sight words*: 'halt', 'wolf'. *Early words*: 'talk', 'walk', 'carpet', 'post', 'roses'.]

Lesson 10   **Review and Post-test**

This Review consolidates the knowledge gained throughout Book 4 as well as elements from the previous three books. [*Sight word*: 'lovely'.]

Lesson 1

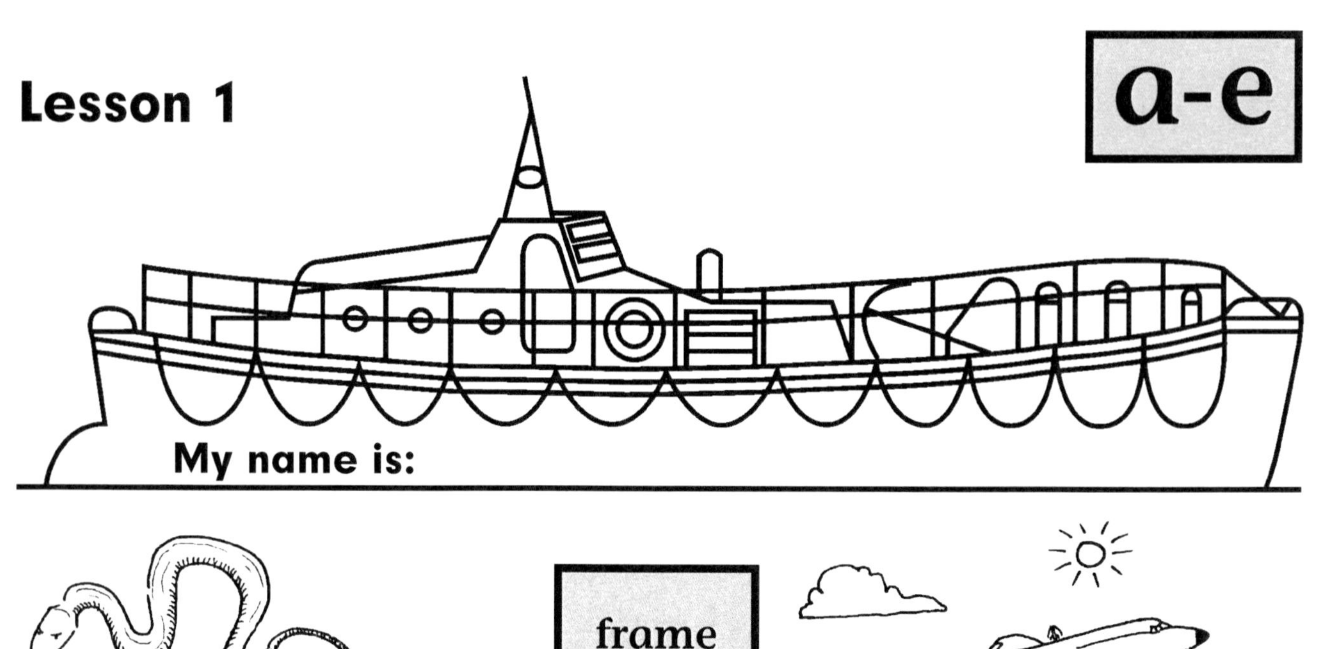

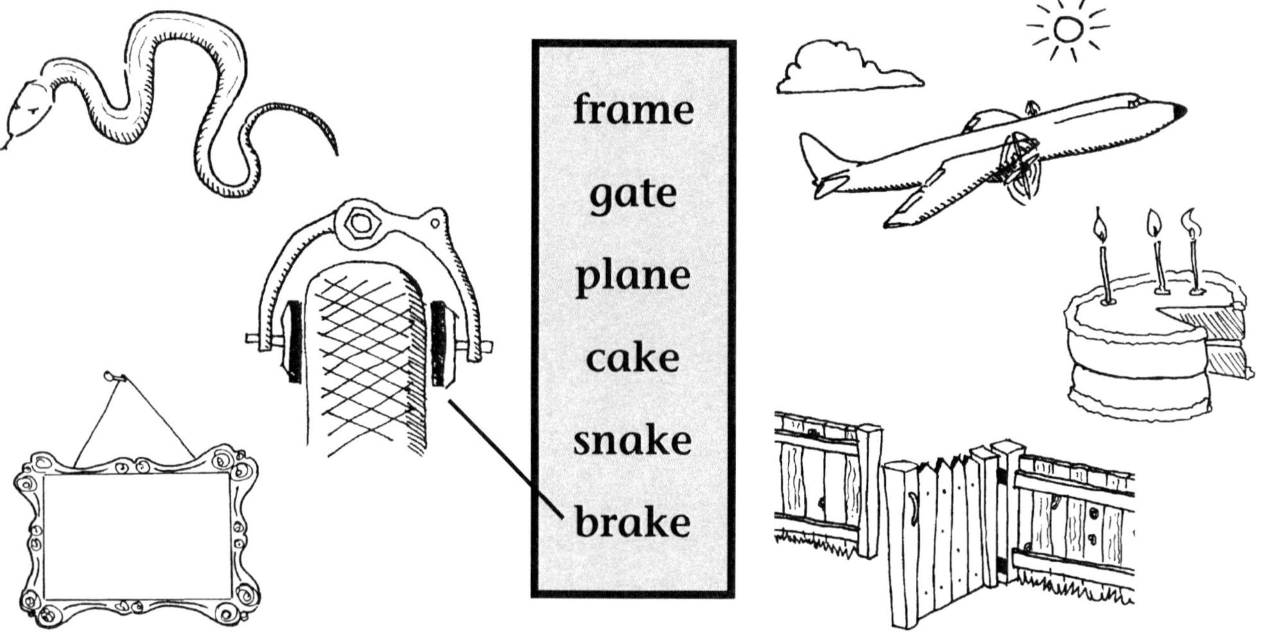

Track: a-e words.

base	case	hill	brake	band
neck	date	snake	snip	make
cape	tale	tap	wave	plane
brave	plant	cake	gate	hiss
mass	tick	mate	crate	plate
glad	glade	rate	brick	dull
bless	lake	ate	cape	ape
strap	cliff	mane	game	cave
cliff	mint	grip	class	lake

Word Match

Circle the same word.

1	**cake**	take	cap	(cake)	cane
2	**gate**	date	grate	grit	gate
3	**cape**	cap	cape	cut	clap
4	**plane**	plan	prick	plastic	plane
5	**tale**	tape	late	tale	tent
6	**gave**	gave	glade	wave	wade
7	**crane**	came	can	crane	plane
8	**snake**	sake	snack	snake	slack

Spell and Write

Circle the letters. Write the word.

#	Letters	Picture	Word
1	(c) k (a) e (ke) te		*cake*
2	g c e a te pe		
3	bl pl a i me ne		
4	fr t a e se me		
5	st sn i a ke ce		
6	n m a e le ne		
7	br dr e a ke te		
8	t sl a i de pe		

Book 4 | Lesson 1 | Page 3

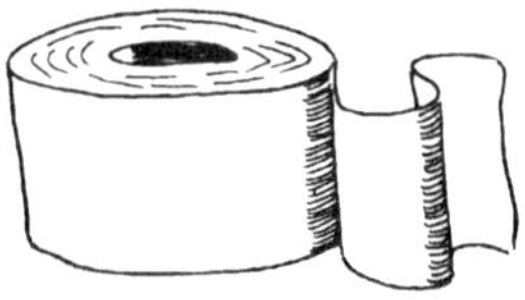

1	◯ The cake had a bell on it.	✓ The cake fell in the lake.
2	◯ Fred had a date with Jan.	◯ Fred had to take the tape to Jan.
3	◯ The plane was late.	◯ The plane was made of plastic.
4	◯ We gave Sam a snack at the picnic.	◯ Sam gave the tent a kick.
5	◯ The snake slid in the crate.	◯ We had to wake the snake in the crate.
6	◯ Tame the cat with the big mane.	◯ Tame the cat to sit on your lap.
7	◯ Scruff the dog came up the lane.	◯ Scruff is the cat's name.

1   Fred had a date with Scruff the dog.

2   The crab gave a wave to his mate.

3   The kite had a red strand made of plastic.

4   Cross the lake to get to the gate.

5   Snuff the dog made a kid late for a date.

Handwriting – copy neatly.

ate

take

game

brave

Circle the odd one out. **Underline** the same.

1	<u>make</u>	<u>cake</u>	(cape)
2	date	take	rate
3	game	same	cane
4	made	mate	glade
5	crate	plane	lane
6	blade	wade	blame
7	crane	cape	cane
8	fade	spade	tale
9	lane	lame	dame
10	plane	Jane	fame

1   Ben can make a _______________ in the tin.

2   Sam had a _______________ with Kim.

3   We can play the _______________ of hide and find.

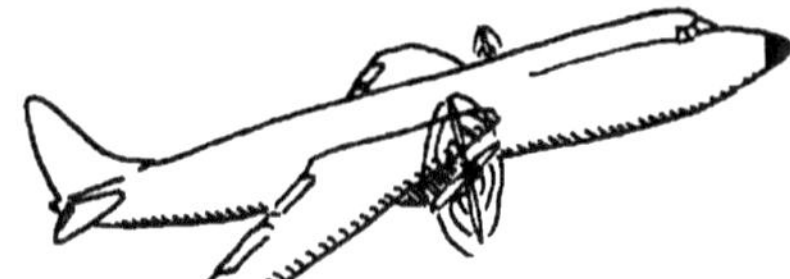

4   We go on a _______________ to the USA.

5   A _______________ is a big pond.

6   Jim _______________ a tin man to _______________ back to class.

7   We pack the _______________ with lots of flakes.

Use these words to complete the sentences.

crate	cake	made	date
game	plane	lake	take

q	t	e	r	u	m	t	o	g	r
f	a	d	b	r	a	k	e	l	k
a	p	e	s	n	k	c	x	a	x
k	e	g	m	h	e	p	b	d	g
e	c	f	c	a	v	e	h	e	h
x	m	a	a	t	e	g	x	d	l
b	n	a	p	e	n	g	a	g	a
n	z	f	v	e	b	p	s	m	k
c	a	m	e	x	h	t	a	m	e
h	d	a	t	e	t	a	l	e	f
f	z	a	g	b	w	v	e	n	m

Find these words.

ape	ate	brake	came	cape	cave
date	game	glade	hate	sale	tame
tape	tale	lake	nape	make	fake

Lesson 2

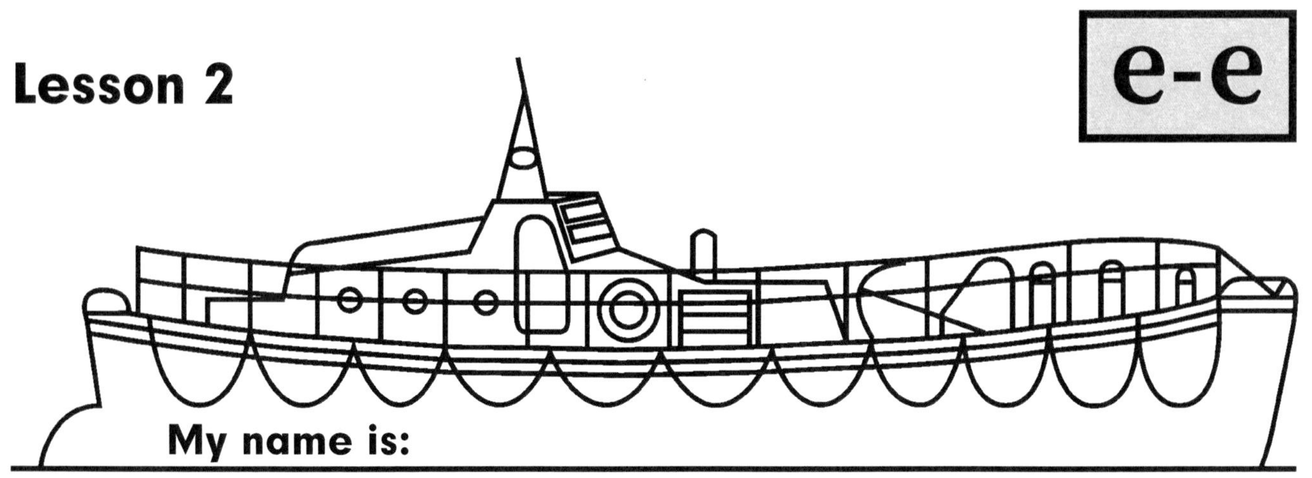

Chinese
here
Steve
swede
stampede
compete
complete

Track: e-e words.

Steve →	are	pine	here	elect
fill	gave	mere	tug	ate
mine	Steve	mane	concrete	theme
end	he	eve	kite	even
fate	cape	interfere	male	made
compete	mine	cut	complete	slave
stampede	extreme	us	small	step
stick	athlete	stop	hop	swede

Book 4 | Lesson 2 | Page 1

Word Match

Circle the same word.

1	**compete**	compare	complete	(compete)	Pete
2	**here**	hot	rest	her	here
3	**these**	their	these	his	hem
4	**eve**	vent	even	here	eve
5	**Steve**	Steven	stop	Steve	step
6	**swede**	swede	wed	west	sand
7	**complete**	compete	plate	complete	comic
8	**mere**	here	mere	Eve	mine

Spell and Write

Circle the letters. Write the word.

1	(h) f a (e) (re) me	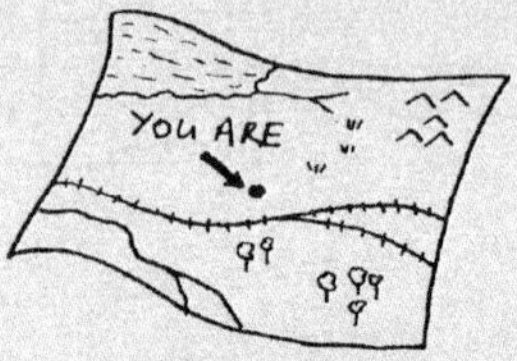	*here*
2	Chi th i ne se te		
3	con com a pe te re		
4	stam sted a pe de te		
5	con cos cre a de te		
6	sh sw e a de te	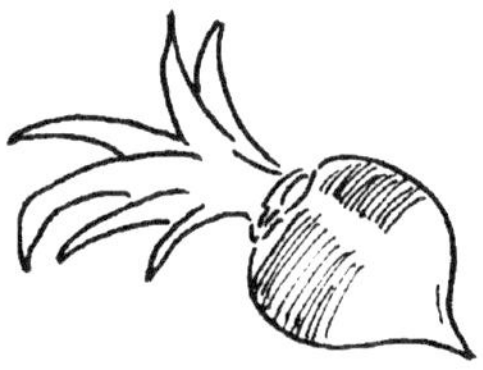	
7	E n e v te e	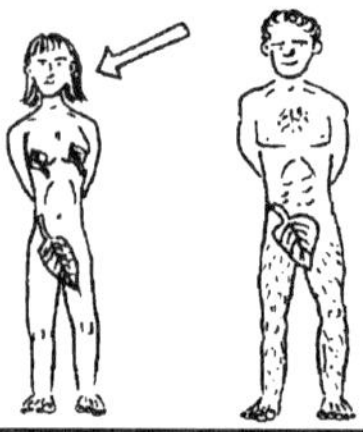	
8	th com e ple te me	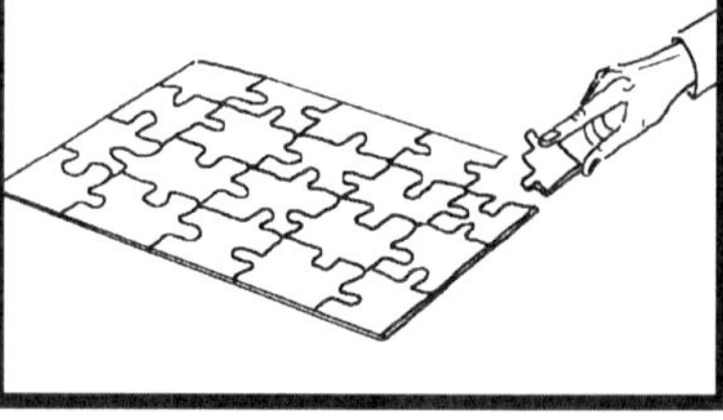	

Book 4 | Lesson 2 | Page 3

1	✓ The concrete will not set.		◯ Do you like my red concrete?
2	◯ My name is Steve.		◯ My name is Sally.
3	◯ Here is your gold belt.		◯ Your gold belt is lost.
4	◯ We are here.		◯ Batman rides his pony.
5	◯ Complete the sum here.	$5 + ? = 10$	◯ To complete the sum you must add on five.
6	◯ Try and compete in the race.		◯ It is too late to compete in the race.
7	◯ Steve hid the swede.		◯ We like swedes.

1   Will Steve mix the concrete here?

____

2   Try to compete and complete the test.

____

3   With these cakes I will get fat.

____

4   On the eve of Christmas the tree was full of gifts.

____

Handwriting – copy neatly.

here

eve

swede

complete

Circle the odd one out. **Underline** the same.

1	compete	complete	common
2	Chinese	these	eve
3	small	here	hall
4	mere	here	these
5	here	eve	Steve
6	complete	met	compete
7	these	this	miss
8	tent	extreme	bent
9	hiss	kiss	here
10	met	mere	let

1   The lad is _____________ on the hill.

2   Let us scrub the _____________.

3   On the eve of his test _____________ was ill.

4   I will _____________ the big job.

5   You _____________ in a fun run.

6   _____________ fell off the tall wall.

Use these words to complete the sentences.

concrete	here	Eve	Steve
	complete	compete	

Wordsearch

m	a	l	n	t	h	e	l	e	o
c	e	z	m	g	S	t	e	v	e
o	d	r	q	e	s	t	x	u	t
n	f	h	e	r	e	w	t	f	h
c	g	c	t	e	v	y	e	j	e
r	c	o	m	p	e	t	e	d	v
e	h	v	p	a	h	e	m	e	e
t	j	s	p	i	e	s	e	f	n
e	c	o	m	p	l	e	t	e	v
p	k	b	r	f	c	v	b	n	x
s	t	a	m	p	e	d	e	e	r

Find these words.

Steve	eve	here	compete
complete	stampede	swede	mere
	even	concrete	

Lesson 3

fl fr gl gr

Track: fl, gr.

(flog) →	grab	black	slap	glad	slug	frost
flab	pram	snap	frill	spin	glint	grill
drag	fled	plum	from	plan	flit	trap
grass	drip	glum	clan	flack	nest	grant
clap	flock	stub	grand	stun	frog	fist
glide	mist	tram	flip	slap	trip	grip
grit	slug	flint	dust	glass	stop	fret
drat	gram	stun	frantic	bred	flick	snug
grim	fly	flat	glade	rest	frock	slop
grasp	best	land	mint	flap	from	gran

Word Match

1	**flag**	from	flick	(flag)	plug
2	**frog**	glad	frog	flan	pram
3	**glad**	glade	grand	glad	glum
4	**flop**	flog	flip	fled	flop
5	**gram**	gran	gram	grip	pram
6	**glass**	gloss	grass	toss	glass
7	**frost**	frost	from	frock	frill
8	**grass**	gloss	glass	grass	glen

Spell and Write

Circle the letters. Write the word.

1	(fl) fr (a) e k (g)	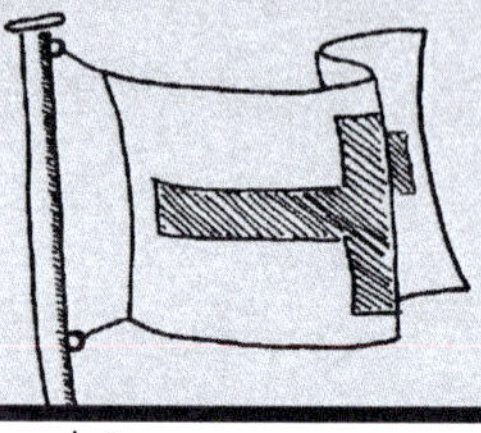 *flag*
2	fr gr o e k g	
3	fr fl u o st sp	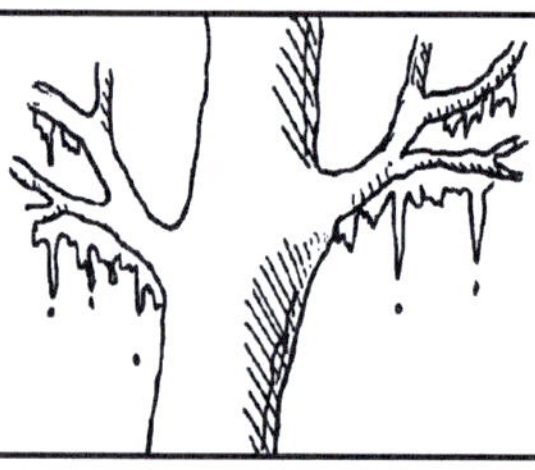
4	bl gl a o b d	
5	gr pr e a ss st	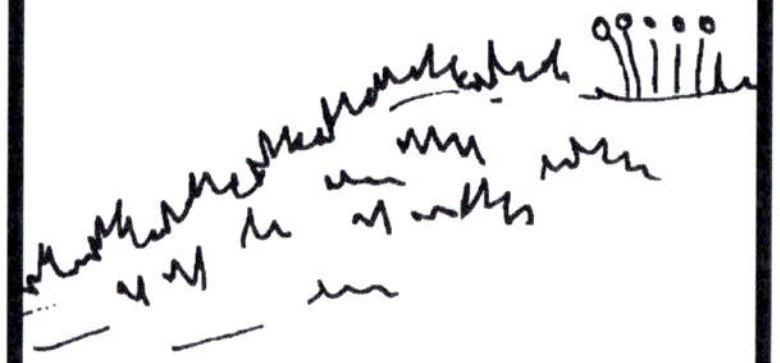
6	gr gl i o de be	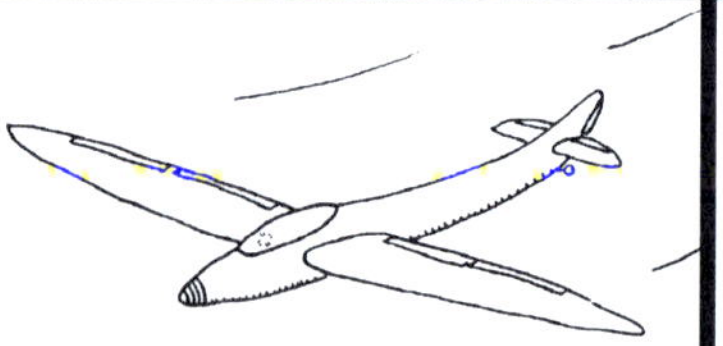
7	gl gr e i n m	
8	fl fr e a p g	

Read and Choose

1	○ I was glad to see the flag fly on the mast.		✓ The flag was lost from the mast.
2	○ The frog hid in the grass.		○ Tom went to grab the frog.
3	○ The glass made a glint in the sun.		○ I can grin into the glass.
4	○ Grandad fled to the dog pen.	 CAMP	○ Grandad was frantic when he lost his tent.
5	○ My flat mate is Tom.		○ My flat mate ate a big cake.
6	○ The frost made the frog flip.		○ The frost made the land crisp.
7	○ Grandma had a big grin.		○ Grandad had a big grin.

1   The glad frog came from the grass.

2   The man had frostbite and was glum.

3   Grandad had a fine grip of the kite.

4   Grant was glad to go from the grasslands.

5   My mate has a flat in Finland.

Handwriting – copy neatly.

fl

fr

gl

gr

Circle the odd one out. Underline the same.

1	<u>gl</u>ad	(gram)	<u>gl</u>ib
2	flag	flog	frog
3	grab	glad	grub
4	flick	frost	from
5	fret	flap	flit
6	grit	glass	grass
7	glade	glide	grime
8	flatmate	frantic	frostbite
9	grin	gland	grand
10	frock	flick	flame

1   The _____________ had to hop onto the _____________.

2   Sam's _____________ lost his kite.

3   The man was _____________ to bake a cake.

4   A _____________ was up the mast.

5   The plane can _____________.

6   The grass was lost in the _____________ and _____________.

7   Tom likes his egg _____________.

Use these words to complete the sentences.

flan	glad	frog	grandad
flag	grass	glide	frost	fog

Wordsearch

g	r	a	m	g	l	a	n	d	a
r	b	d	f	g	l	a	s	s	f
a	g	i	f	r	a	n	t	i	c
b	j	g	l	a	o	k	m	o	g
g	g	r	a	n	d	s	o	n	l
f	l	a	b	d	f	r	t	m	a
r	i	i	f	l	a	t	u	w	d
o	d	f	d	f	l	o	c	k	h
m	e	r	o	e	l	f	r	o	g
g	l	e	n	g	l	o	s	s	t
f	g	r	i	t	i	p	p	g	s

Find these words.

glad	grit	flab	glide	grand	glass
frantic	frost	flat	flock	flop	frog
from	glen	gloss	gram	gland	grab

Lesson 4 {o-e}

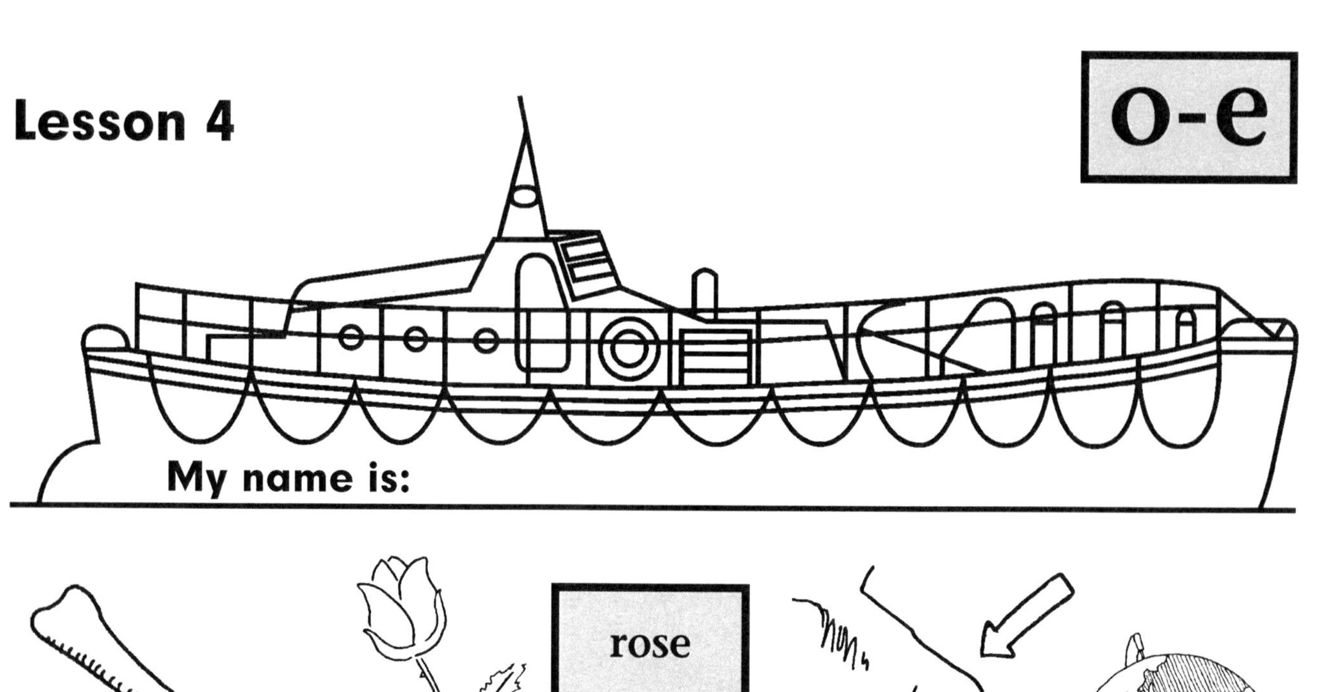

Track: o-e words.

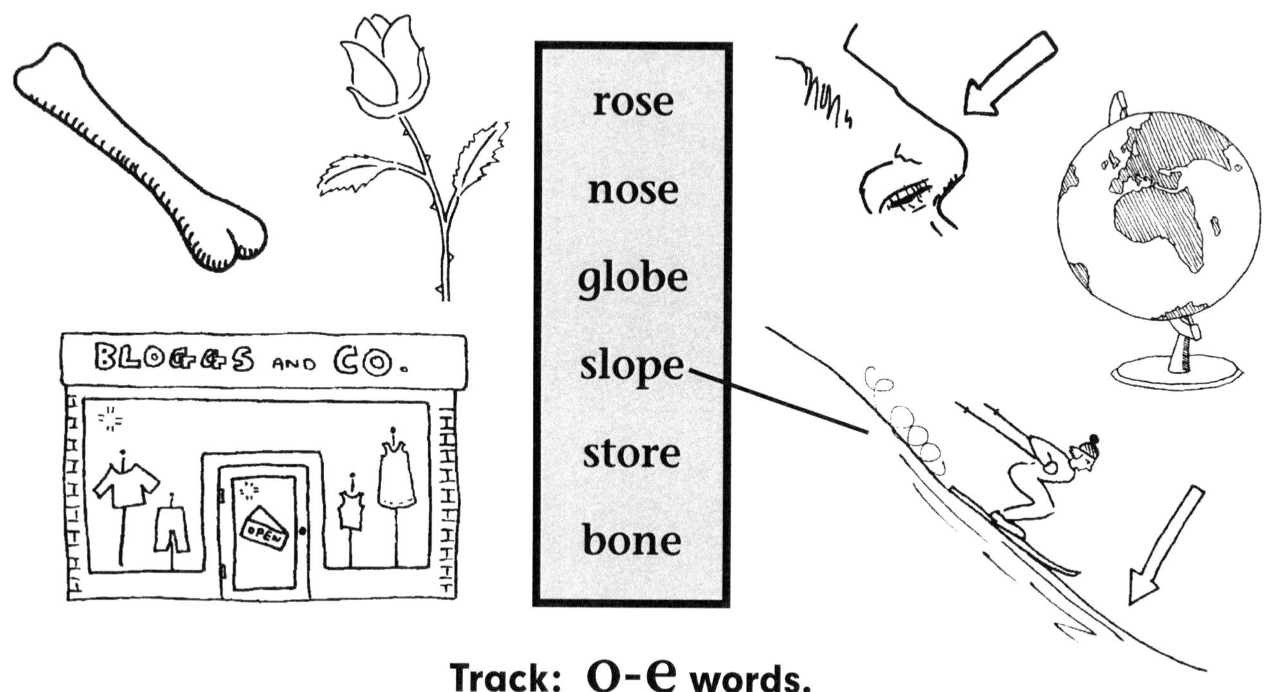

ape	bone	trade	cone	ball	nose
spade	slope	stone	time	strode	cake
swell	close	ride	sit	poke	make
pole	plane	attic	mole	line	lick
broke	life	hope	blade	basic	stole
it	tape	pride	hole	line	home
panic	coke	take	hide	cope	dale
lone	fade	pope	note	stile	stake

Book 4 | Lesson 4 | Page 1

Word Match

Circle the same word.

1	**nose**	rose	note	(nose)	not
2	**globe**	glade	glad	lobe	globe
3	**bone**	bond	bone	blade	block
4	**hope**	hope	hop	hole	pole
5	**poke**	pope	joke	bake	poke
6	**broke**	brake	broke	drake	bloke
7	**stone**	scone	step	stone	slope
8	**rope**	hope	rope	hole	cope

Spell and Write

Circle the letters. Write the word.

1	m o se	n a ke	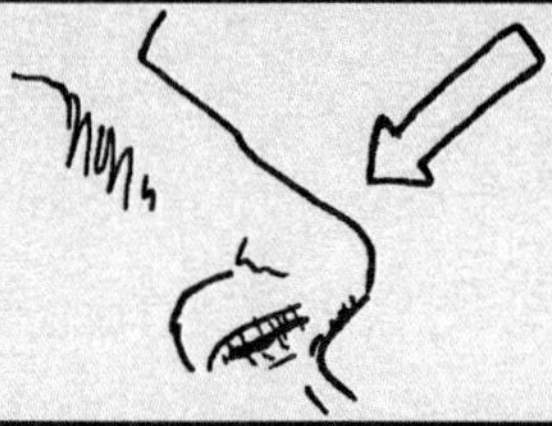	nose
2	k i ne	c o me		
3	d o me	b e ne		
4	gl o de	cl a be		
5	n a te	m o pe		
6	w o se	r i te		
7	sl a pe	sc o de		
8	k o pe	r i te	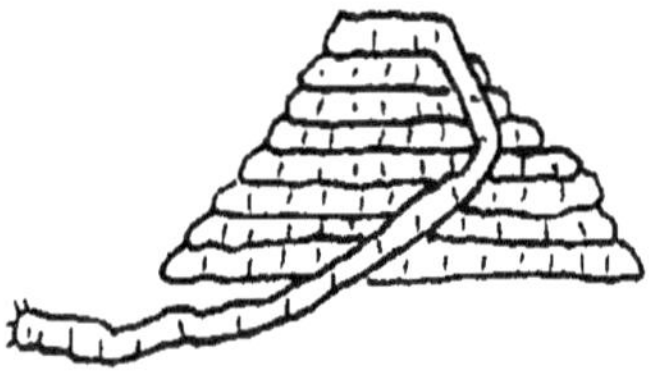	

Read and Choose

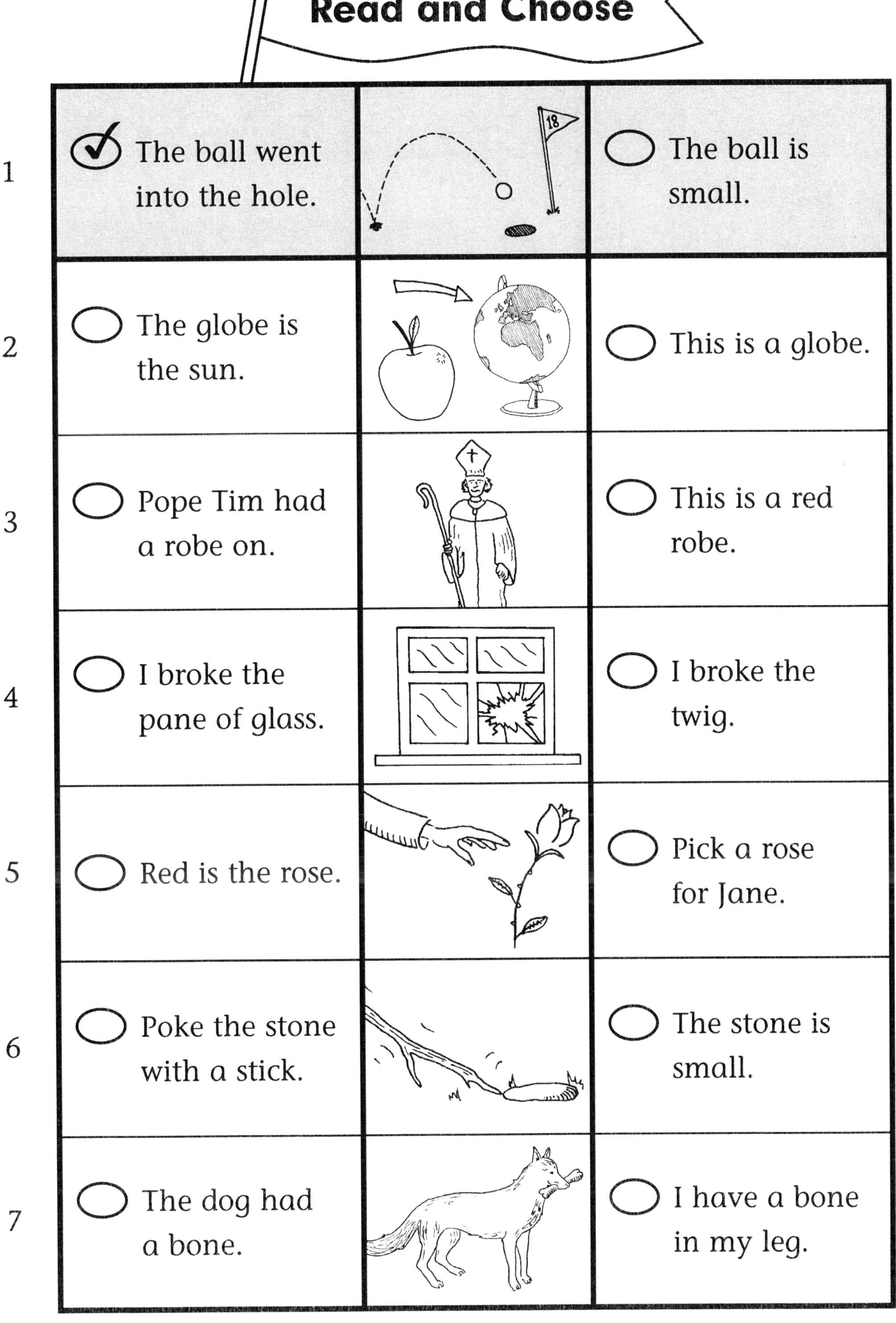

1	✓ The ball went into the hole.		◯ The ball is small.
2	◯ The globe is the sun.		◯ This is a globe.
3	◯ Pope Tim had a robe on.		◯ This is a red robe.
4	◯ I broke the pane of glass.		◯ I broke the twig.
5	◯ Red is the rose.		◯ Pick a rose for Jane.
6	◯ Poke the stone with a stick.		◯ The stone is small.
7	◯ The dog had a bone.		◯ I have a bone in my leg.

1   Sam's nose is black and wet.

2   Roll the ball on the grass just by the bone.

3   I hope we are close to home.

4   Up the slope we go.

5   The mole dug a hole in the hill.

Handwriting – copy neatly.

globe

Rome

rose

note

Circle the odd one out. **Underline** the same.

1	<u>rose</u>	(cone)	<u>nose</u>
2	stone	bone	slope
3	broke	dose	coke
4	robe	globe	strode
5	lone	mole	hole
6	robe	hope	cope
7	sole	mole	note
8	rose	pose	sole
9	slope	stroke	pope
10	spoke	stoke	stone

1   The dog sat on the ________________.

2   Tony ________________ his leg.

3   ________________ the gate behind you.

4   This ________________ was dug by a ________________.

5   The ________________ has a smell.

6   Go up the ________________ to the top.

7   Take this ________________ to your mum.

Use these words to complete the sentences.

| slope | mole | hole | broke |
| note | Close | bone | rose |

Book 4 | Lesson 4 | Page 7

h	o	l	e	q	g	p	v	t	u
r	u	n	l	s	l	o	w	k	s
m	p	o	p	e	o	k	v	y	b
m	c	o	n	e	b	e	q	h	o
c	o	k	e	o	e	h	b	n	n
o	d	s	r	o	t	e	l	a	e
p	e	h	h	v	s	e	o	t	q
e	w	o	o	s	t	o	k	e	b
t	s	m	p	p	o	l	e	r	l
u	q	e	e	r	n	e	s	y	u
l	o	n	e	k	e	k	h	m	w

Find these words.

cone	home	stoke	note	cope	pole
coke	poke	lone	stone	hole	globe
bloke	hope	bone	rote	code	pope

Lesson 5

My name is:

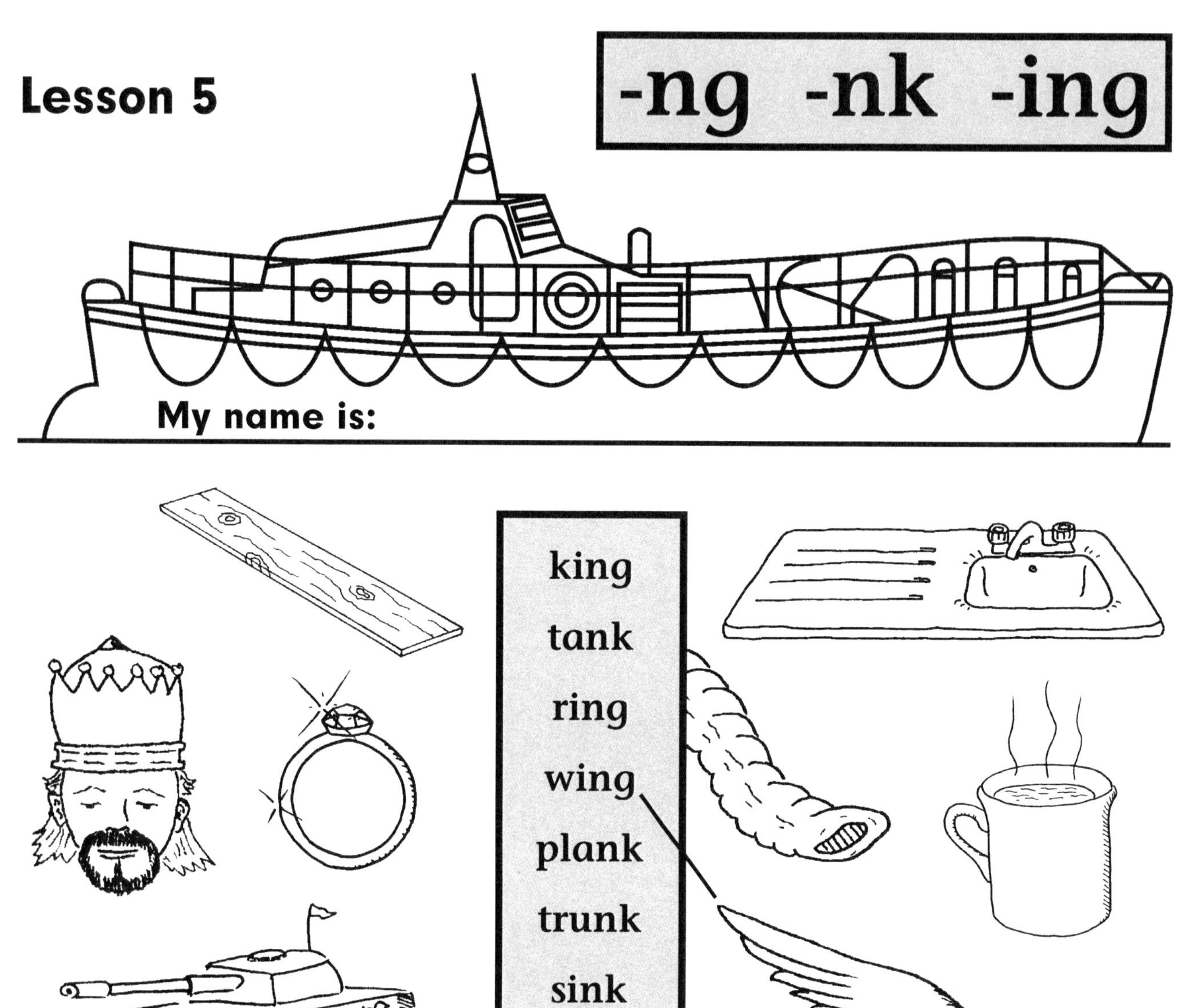

Track: ng, nk.

ng	tr	dr	pl	nk	gl	pt	nd	nt
ng	gr	ng	ic	nk	nd	nk	gr	tr
ng	gh	dr	ng	tr	nk	gh	pr	tr
ng	ut	ng	st	nd	ng	nk	tr	nk
st	nk	sp	tr	ng	sn	sp	nk	tr
ck	sp	nk	tr	ng	tr	up	sn	nk
nt	nd	tr	sp	nk	ng	pr	dr	ng

Word Match

Circle the same word.

1	**king**	sing	wing	(king)	cling
2	**fang**	hang	fang	sang	bang
3	**ring**	ring	sing	sling	ping
4	**drink**	stink	wink	brink	drink
5	**tank**	sank	plank	tank	drank
6	**string**	wing	ring	string	spring
7	**trunk**	drunk	trunk	hunt	bunk
8	ink	sink	pink	link	ink

Spell and Write

Circle the letters. Write the word.

#	Letters	Picture	Word
1	(k) c (i) e nt (ng)		*king*
2	tr dr o u nk ng		
3	tr dr e i nk ng		
4	w r i e ng nk		
5	bl pl a o ng nk		
6	t l e a ng nk		
7	spr str e i ng nk		
8	th f e a ng nk		

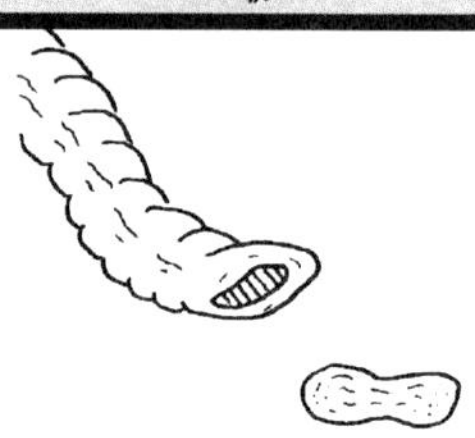

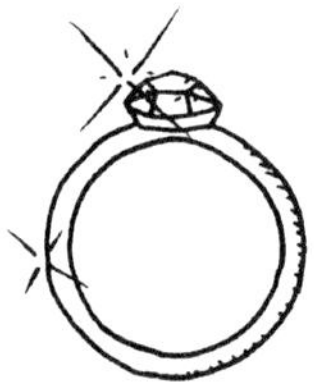

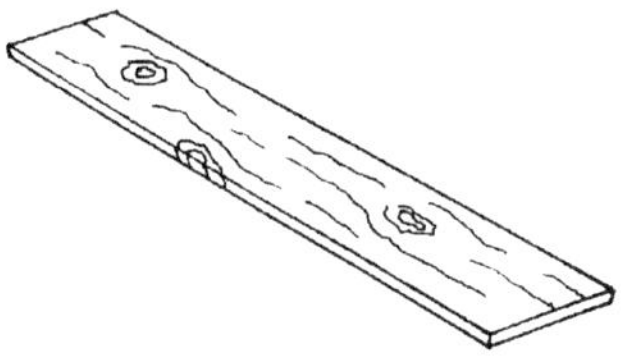

Book 4 | Lesson 5 | Page 3

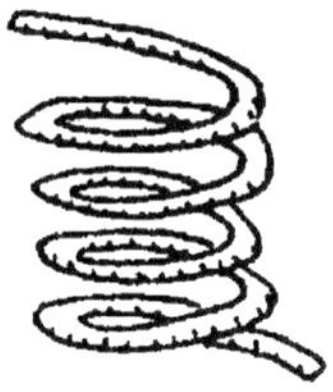

Read and Choose

1	✓ The man stands on the plank.	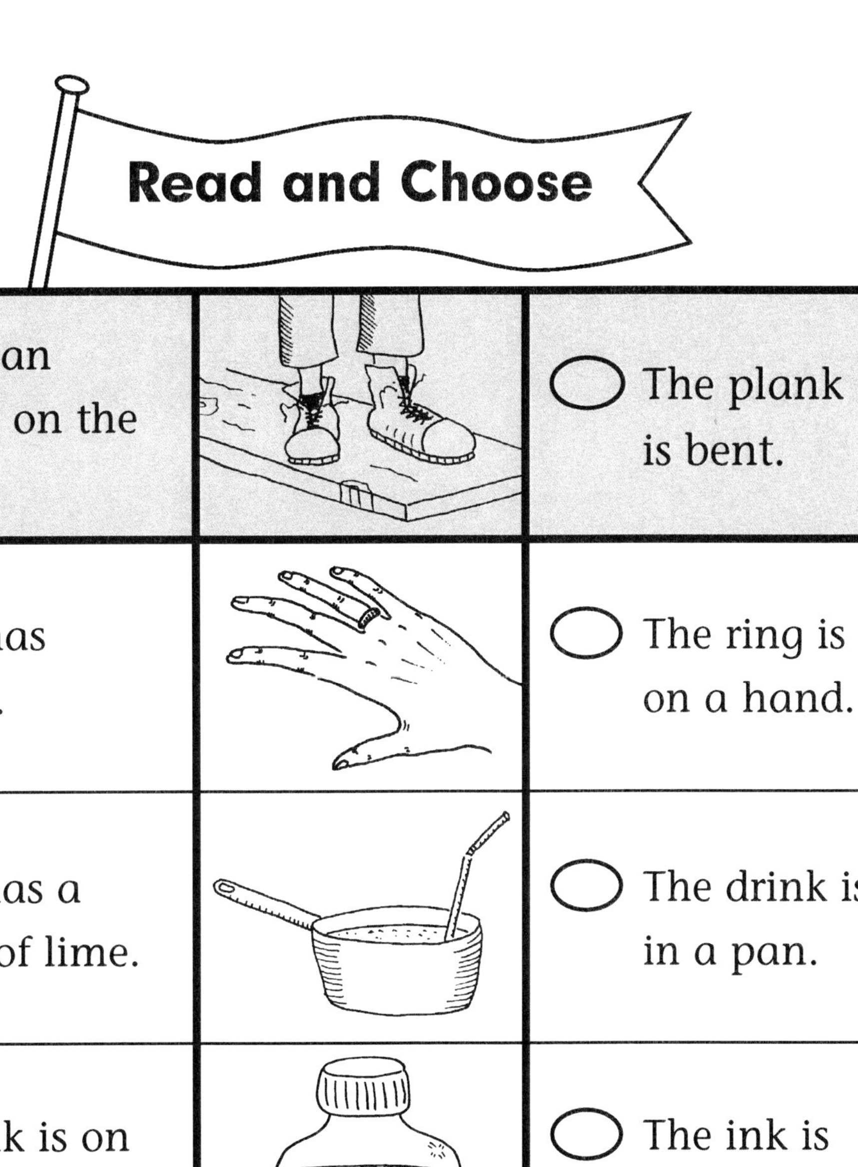	◯ The plank is bent.
2	◯ Pam has a ring.		◯ The ring is on a hand.
3	◯ Sam has a drink of lime.		◯ The drink is in a pan.
4	◯ The ink is on the desk.		◯ The ink is black.
5	◯ Sam is at the sink.		◯ Here are 4 cups in the sink.
6	◯ We can fly with wings.		◯ An ant has wings.
7	◯ The ball of string is small.	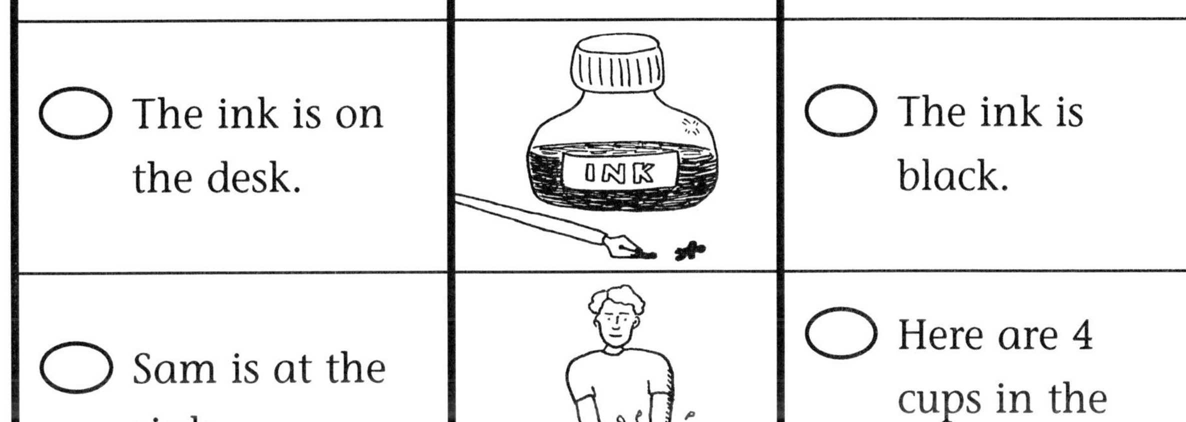	◯ Here are 2 balls of string.

1   The ball of string is pink.

2   Ring the bell to run the tank.

3   Black ink is put in the pen.

4   King Sam has a ring in his hand.

5   Drink all your drink of lime.

Handwriting – copy neatly.

ng

nk

ing

sink

Circle the odd one out. Underline the same.

1	<u>king</u>	(tank)	<u>wing</u>
2	sink	pink	ring
3	sang	sink	slang
4	string	cling	wink
5	tank	fang	bank
6	drink	sing	wing
7	ink	sink	long
8	plank	song	sank
9	tank	hang	sprang
10	long	song	sank

1   Ken puts _____________ in his pen.

2   Cups are put in the _____________.

3   The string is very _____________.

4   _____________ Tom is _____________.

5   The _____________ is in Jan's hand.

6   We _____________ a lively _____________ at the Grand Hotel.

Use these words to complete the sentences.

sang	ink	song	sink
long	King	strong	ring

Book 4 | Lesson 5 | Page 7

Wordsearch

b	a	n	k	f	a	n	k	o	t
l	t	e	s	l	a	n	g	h	t
a	u	c	k	i	t	n	u	n	k
n	s	l	i	n	g	a	g	g	e
k	s	i	n	g	a	o	n	s	n
l	o	n	g	u	s	e	t	k	t
h	i	g	o	n	g	i	o	n	k
s	a	n	g	p	l	a	n	k	o
t	o	o	r	i	n	g	k	k	n
u	v	l	o	n	g	g	a	n	c
k	o	v	l	g	w	i	n	g	e

Find these words.

king	tank	sling	plank	long	sink
ring	cling	wing	sing	ping	fling
fang	gong	slang	bank	blank	sang

Lesson 6

Track: ire, ore.

stare	wire	spire	care	score
dare	hire	more	step	wore
bare	core	scare	tore	bang
strap	tins	spore	rare	lines
tire	dent	Clare	pore	time
lanes	click	hire	glare	dire
blameless	fire	trick	fling	snore
spring	Batman	robin	bore	sore

Word Match

Circle the same word.

1	**score**	stone	tore	core	(score)
2	**dare**	bare	Clare	dare	stare
3	**hire**	wine	tire	fine	hire
4	**more**	core	snore	more	wore
5	**stare**	scare	stare	Clare	glare
6	**wire**	wire	hire	spire	tire
7	**wore**	more	wore	bore	fore
8	**care**	care	Clare	dare	rare

Spell and Write

Circle the letters. Write the word.

1	(sp) bl / ore (ire)		_spire_
2	c k / ore are		____________
3	w m / are ire	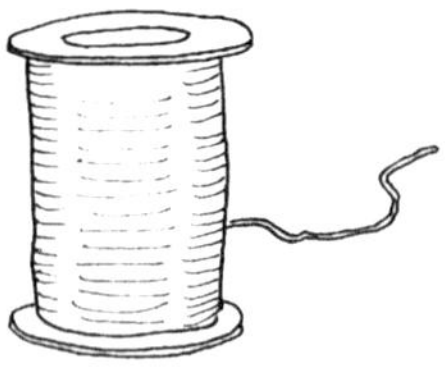	____________
4	c f / ire ore		____________
5	sk sc / ore are	 SMITH 15 / JONES 12	____________
6	st sp / ere are		____________
7	h f / ire are		____________
8	n m / ore are		____________

Read and Choose

1	✔ The bus fare is 15p.	What is the bus fare?
2	◯ Smoke from the fire is black.	◯ The fire is red hot.
3	◯ Pat has more cake than I have.	◯ Tone has more wine in his glass.
4	◯ The score at the game was 2-5.	◯ At the end of the game the score was nil.
5	◯ At the top of the spire was a cat.	◯ A brass cross was on top of the spire.
6	◯ Do not scare the old black mare.	◯ The mare has a hare on her back.
7	◯ We can hire a bike from the store.	◯ The wine will cost more at the store.

1   The fire was in the spire.

2   The bus fare for Clare was more than 15p.

3   Pat had to care for the sick mare.

4   There is a store from where you can hire a bike.

5   It is rare to see a hare on top of a spire.

Handwriting – copy neatly.

ire

are

ore

care

(Circle) the odd one out. Underline the same.

1	<u>score</u>	(spire)	<u>snore</u>
2	hare	mare	pore
3	wire	more	hire
4	core	stare	glare
5	more	mare	wore
6	tore	tire	spire
7	dare	bore	bare
8	bare	hare	hire
9	stare	core	snore
10	fire	hire	fare

Cloze Procedure

1   At the top of the _______________ is a cat.

2   Put the _______________ in the bin.

3   The _______________ is very hot.

4   Do not _______________ at the strong lad.

5   Can I have some _______________ drink?

6   Take _______________ not to fall from the wall.

7   The bus _______________ home is 15p.

8   There is a big _______________ at the top of the lane.

Use these words to complete the sentences.

stare	more	core	spire
fire	care	fare	store

Wordsearch

t	s	b	a	r	e	s	c	o	n
s	n	o	r	e	s	t	a	r	e
h	m	r	a	h	p	o	r	e	h
t	v	e	r	c	o	r	e	f	a
w	i	r	e	o	r	e	t	i	r
s	w	m	o	r	e	h	i	r	e
s	d	a	r	e	m	a	r	e	h
e	p	r	r	s	p	a	r	e	a
a	r	i	t	e	r	e	r	p	r
q	b	c	r	h	f	m	l	e	e
e	p	g	n	e	o	i	d	k	j

Find these words.

snore	bore	rare	stare	store	spire
pore	hire	more	core	care	bare
ore	mare	dare	spare	ware	hare

Lesson 7

u-e

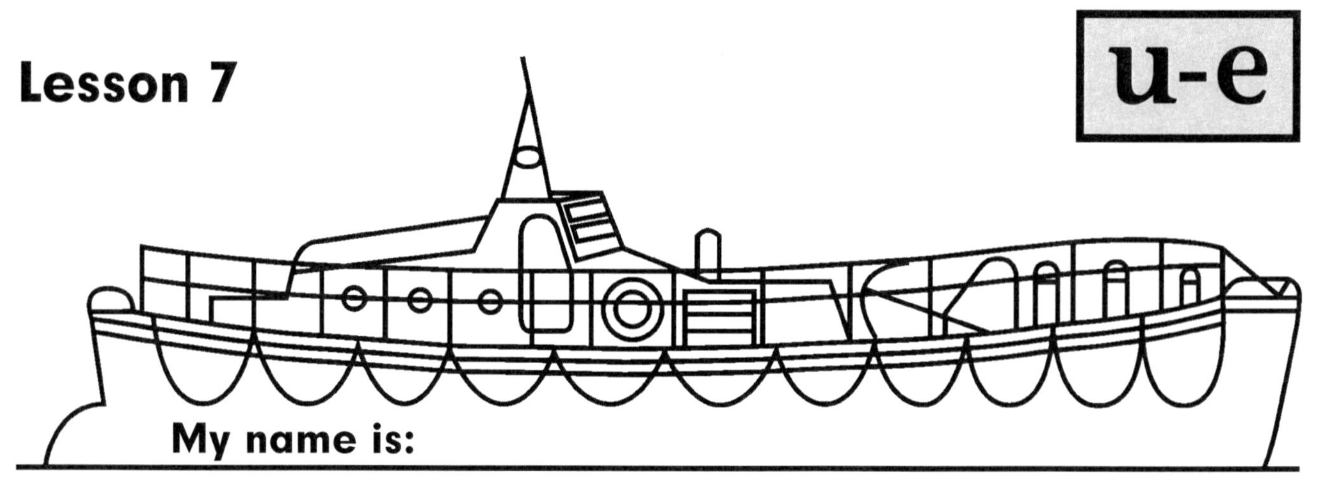

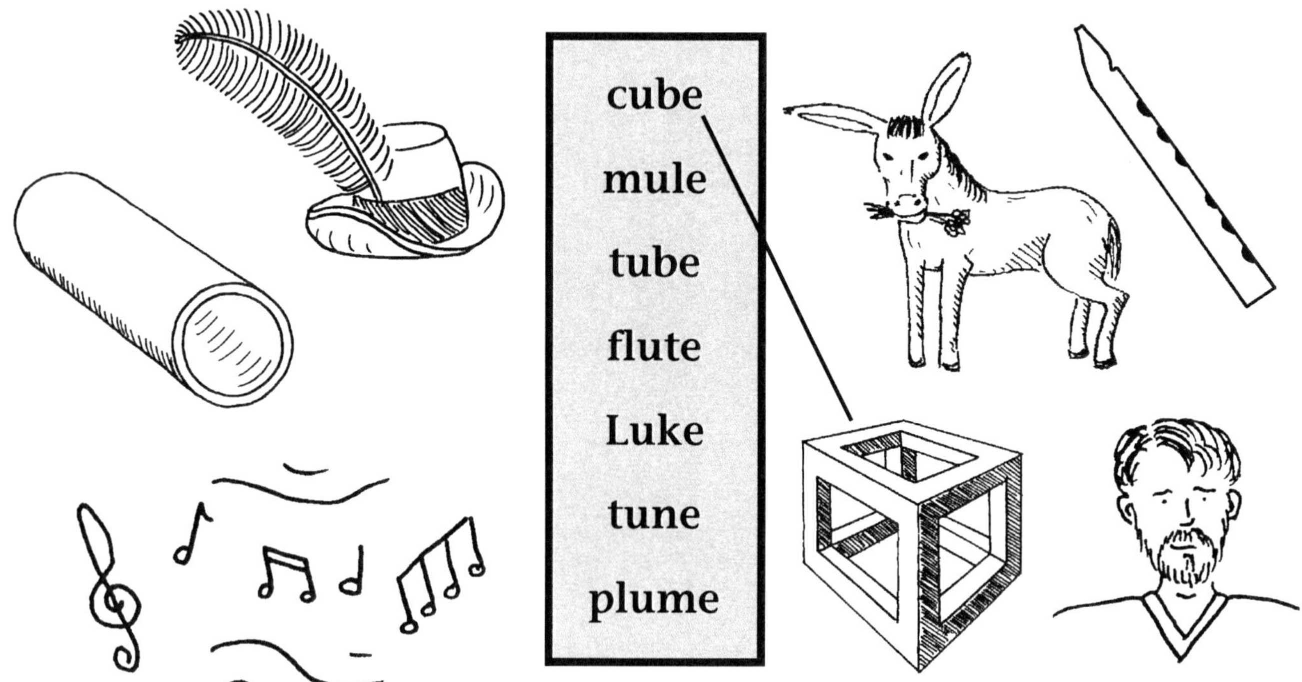

Track: u-e words.

Jane	cube	bone	kite	cute	save
globe	Duke	lake	slope	time	prune
nose	still	Dave	here	fuse	trade
Luke	mule	complete	tube	eve	tape
tune	skate	use	stone	cake	plume
cone	rose	flute	plate	costume	amuse
estate	broke	compete	stampede	dune	tank

Word Match

1	**cube**	cute	cake	(cube)	coke
2	**flute**	inflate	flute	flat	flick
3	**cute**	cube	snake	cope	cute
4	**plume**	plume	pope	spade	pane
5	**dune**	duke	dame	date	dune
6	**tune**	tape	tune	top	tip
7	**tube**	tune	time	tube	tub
8	**fuse**	flute	fuse	fate	fat

Spell and Write

Circle the letters. Write the word.

1	(t) s / (u) a / ce (be)	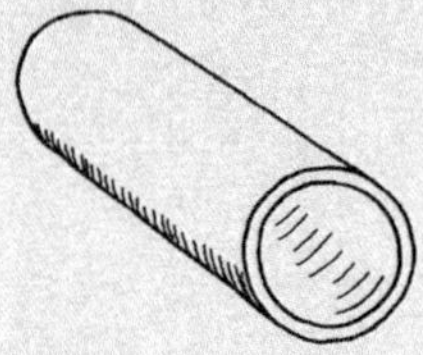	*tube*
2	fl bl / o u / te se		
3	spl pl / u a / te me	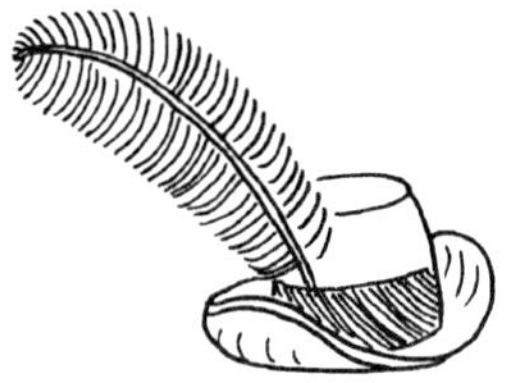	
4	c s / e u / te be	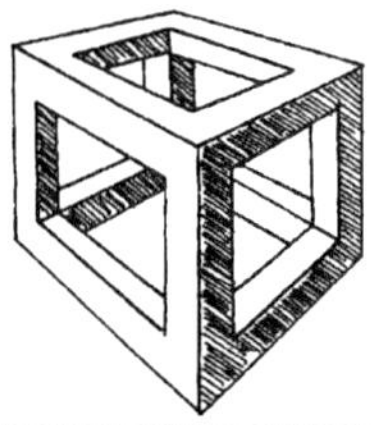	
5	t sp / i u / ne te		
6	L t / a u / te ke		
7	d t / u e / ke ne		
8	t f / u i / be se	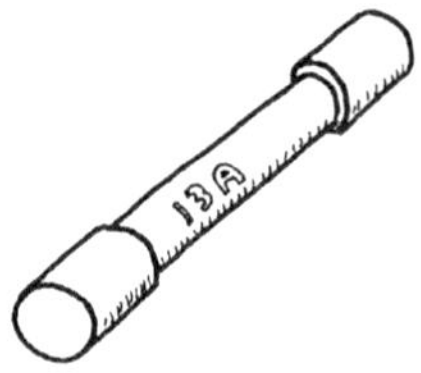	

62

Book 4 | Lesson 7 | Page 3

Read and Choose

1	◯ The man has his flute.	✓ The man has his drum.
2	◯ Sam sits on the ball.	◯ Sam rides the mule.
3	◯ Tim runs with the stick.	◯ Tim is lost in the sand dunes.
4	◯ Fred sat on a cube.	◯ Fred sat on a rock.
5	◯ We can ride on the tube in London.	◯ We can ride on bikes on the grass.
6	◯ Jack sings a tune.	◯ Jill sings a tune.
7	◯ The plug has a fuse.	◯ The plug sits on the mat.

1   Sam and June are lost in the sand dunes.

2   I cannot ride a mule on the tube.

3   Rule a line at the top.

4   The fuse in the plug fits well.

5   Jack made a cube from tin and tape.

Handwriting – copy neatly.

use

cube

flute

rule

Circle the odd one out. Underline the same.

1	<u>flute</u>	(bake)	<u>cute</u>
2	nape	tune	tape
3	fuse	fate	use
4	date	dune	tune
5	rude	crude	cute
6	fuse	mule	rule
7	tube	prune	cube
8	June	tune	rule
9	cute	jute	joke
10	mate	lute	mute

1   We like to sing the _______________ on the T.V.

2   The _______________ rests on the wide music stand.

3   He lost a _______________ in the long _______________.

4   Jenny the _______________ stands on the grass.

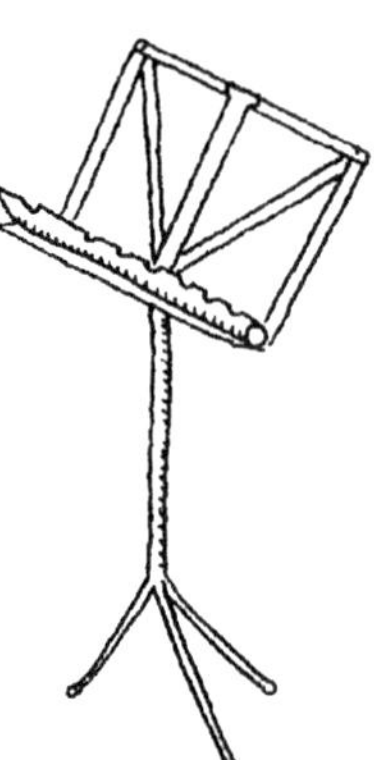

5   Jack and Jill run in the sand _______________.

6   The off-side _______________ stops
     the men running in the game.

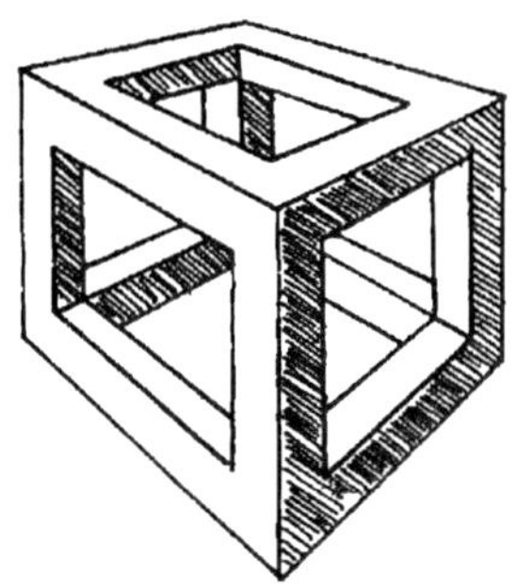

7   A _______________ has six sides.

Use these words to complete the sentences.

cube	tube	flute	tune
mule	dune	rule	fuse

Wordsearch

j	f	l	u	t	e	n	g	s	c
t	u	n	e	k	w	z	a	h	u
u	s	v	x	h	a	f	b	v	b
b	e	n	j	a	c	c	u	s	e
e	l	d	g	u	u	u	s	e	w
p	r	u	n	e	t	t	e	s	x
l	b	k	q	x	e	e	j	f	k
u	h	e	L	u	v	d	j	l	n
m	a	m	u	s	e	m	u	t	e
e	s	z	k	e	k	h	k	n	q
n	m	d	e	w	v	f	e	z	e

Find these words.

fuse	tube	flute	cube	tune	jute
duke	plume	cute	abuse	accuse	acute
Luke	prune	use	amuse	mute	dune

Lesson 8

My name is:

Track: sc, sk.

sc	sp	st	sm	sk	st	sp	sw	sc	sm
st	sc	st	sm	sk	sw	sn	sk	sm	sc
sk	sn	sc	sm	st	sm	sc	sw	sk	sp
sm	sk	sm	st	sk	sp	sw	sc	st	sc
sc	sk	sm	sp	sc	sk	st	sk	sw	sc

Word Match

Circle the same word.

1	**scab**	Scot	scam	(scab)	scum
2	**small**	smut	smog	smell	small
3	**skill**	skip	skin	skill	skim
4	**snag**	snap	snip	snug	snag
5	**swim**	swim	swill	swam	swig
6	**snap**	snob	snap	snip	snag
7	**scum**	scum	Scot	scan	scab
8	**smug**	smog	smut	smoke	smug

Spell and Write

Circle the letters. Write the word.

1	sm u ck	st i g	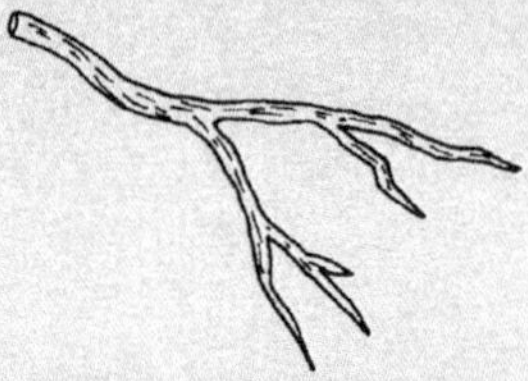	stick
2	sc a p	sm u b	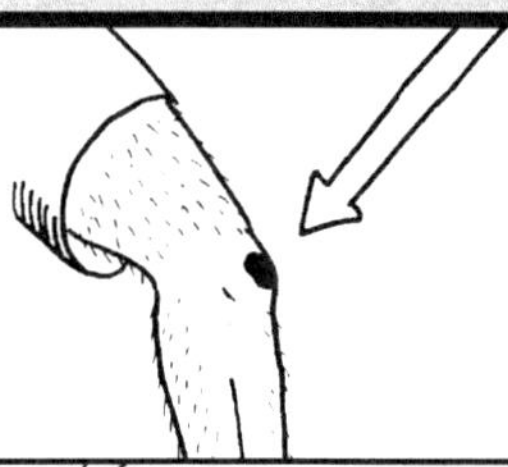	
3	sk e f	sp i p		
4	st e g	sw i p		
5	sn a p	st o ck		
6	spl a d	sk u t		
7	sp o m	sw i d		
8	scr u g	sw i b		

Read and Choose

1	✓ The snake is made up of nuts.		◯ Pam has a snack of nuts.
2	◯ Mac has a scab.		◯ The Scot has a scab on his skin.
3	◯ I can swim in the lake.		◯ The dog can swim in the lake.
4	◯ I can smell the bin.		◯ The bin is as small as an ant.
5	◯ Smog is made from fog and smoke.		◯ Smoke can be black.
6	◯ Tim has a long rope to skip with.		◯ Tim can skip with string.
7	◯ Mum likes to swing rings.		◯ Dad likes to mend rings.

1   The Scot had a scab on his skin.

2   Pam can skip with her rope.

3   The snack has a bad smell.

4   Sam puts ten cubes into a long box.

5   He can swim in the small lake.

Handwriting – copy neatly.

sc

sm

sk

sw

Circle the odd one out. <u>Underline</u> the same.

1	<u>skip</u>	(stop)	<u>skill</u>
2	snap	smell	smut
3	swim	swig	smog
4	step	scab	scale
5	span	skim	skin
6	snug	smug	snag
7	smoke	snack	small
8	scum	skid	spend
9	stop	snip	step
10	snack	spin	spine

Cloze Procedure

1   A ________________ is a man from Scotland.

2   The ________________ is black.

3   Pam has a rope to ________________ with.

4   The ant is so ________________.

5   ________________ the drink from the glass.

6   ________________ the red rose.

7   My ________________ is sore.

8   My mum likes to ________________.

Use these words to complete the sentences.

small	smoke	skip	Scot
Swig	smile	skin	Smell

Book 4 | Lesson 8 | Page 7

Wordsearch

s	m	a	l	l	s	m	e	l	l
k	s	S	t	b	n	a	g	p	a
i	n	c	s	k	i	p	t	v	h
n	a	o	r	s	p	s	w	i	g
s	c	t	s	w	i	m	t	s	u
w	k	s	c	a	l	e	s	c	a
s	s	c	a	m	h	s	m	u	t
s	n	o	b	t	u	h	n	m	s
o	g	t	s	k	i	l	l	u	a
g	t	s	m	o	k	e	h	p	g
a	p	f	i	b	h	g	c	o	m

Find these words.

scab	scum	Scot	scale	scam	small
skip	skill	skin	swam	swim	swig
snob	snip	snack	snug	smoke	smell

Lesson 9

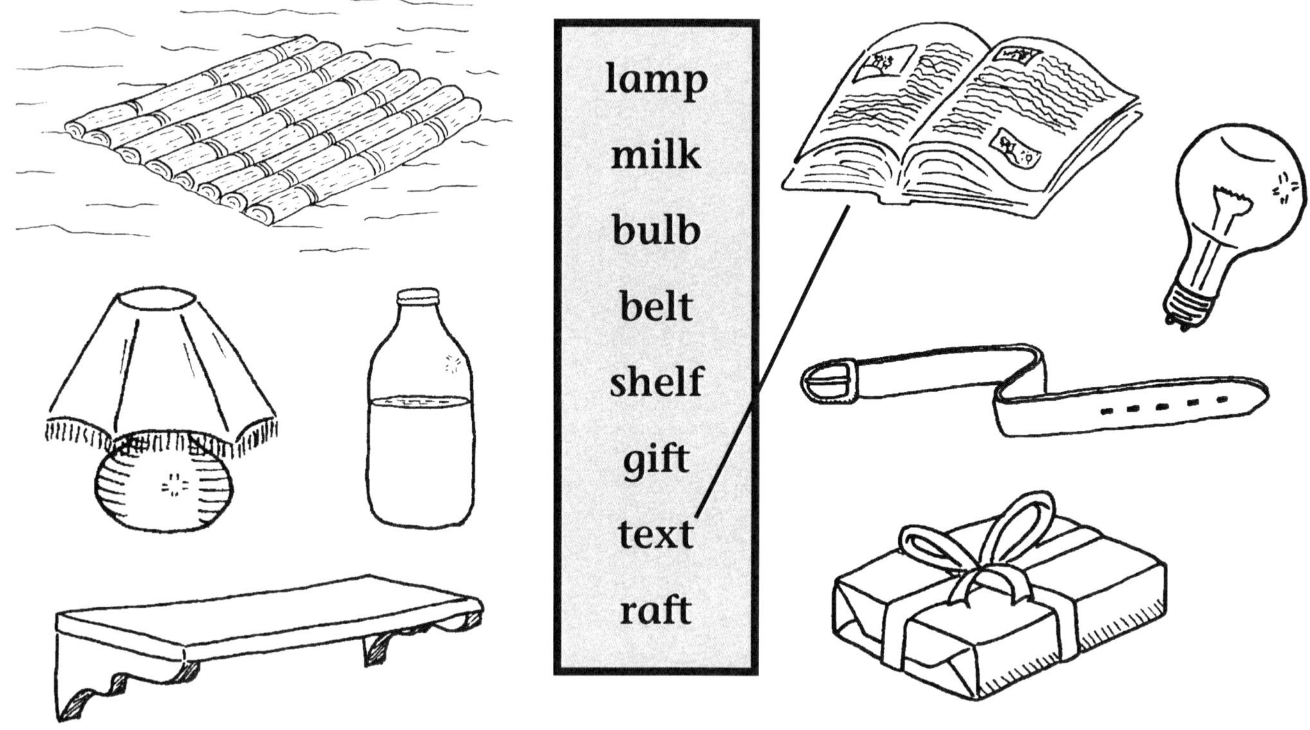

Track: mp, ft.

belt	tramp	bulb	test	call	fact	sift
text	fox	gift	tin	in	self	jug
camp	help	send	mill	fund	clamp	king
silk	wing	jump	smile	raft	time	shelf
stamp	spring	kiss	loft	hare	talk	wilt
hilt	help	miss	cramp	soft	scrape	ramp
walk	told	snap	act	spot	swift	left

Word Match

Circle the same word.

1	**lamp**	limp	clamp	(lamp)	lump
2	**belt**	hilt	halt	bell	belt
3	**swift**	soft	swift	shaft	shift
4	**milk**	walk	silk	milk	elk
5	**tact**	pact	tact	fact	act
6	**bald**	help	stall	ball	bald
7	**self**	self	shelf	wolf	elf
8	**help**	gulp	yelp	help	pulp

Spell and Write

Circle the letters. Write the word.

1	(l) e ft	m (a) (mp)	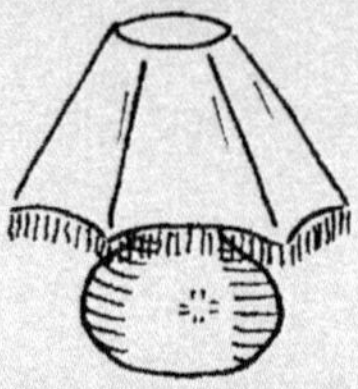	lamp
2	n i lk	m e lt		
3	k a mp	r u lb	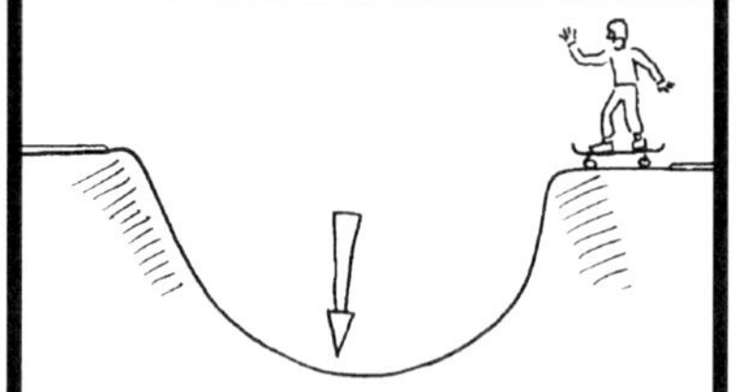	
4	g e ft	j i ct		
5	j u mp	c a lb		
6	d e lk	b i lt	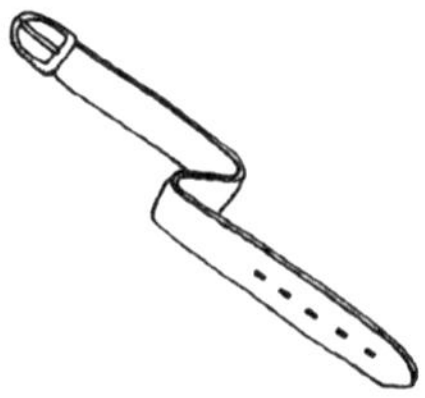	
7	f i ct	th a lk		
8	ch e lf	sh i ft		

Read and Choose

1	✔ The silk piles up on the carpet.	 ◯ The silk is hidden in the loft.
2	◯ It is made of brick.	 ◯ The sun is melting it.
3	◯ No glass is on the shelf.	 ◯ There is a lot of glass on the shelf.
4	◯ The ramp will bump the car.	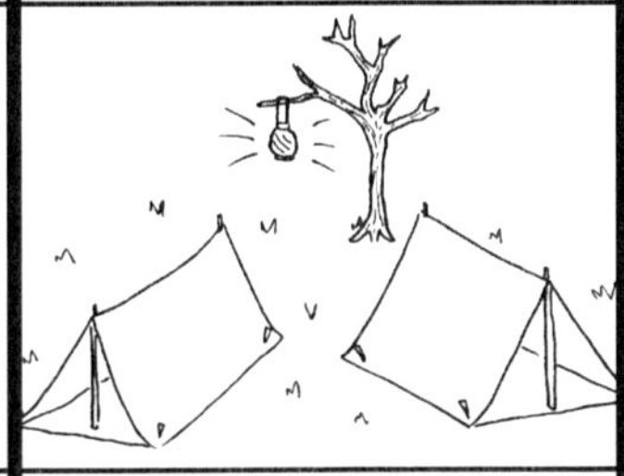 ◯ In the camp was a lamp.
5	◯ In the jug was a splash of milk.	 ◯ The bulk of the milk was fat.
6	◯ The raft was drifting in the lake.	 ◯ The gift was a soft cat.
7	◯ A man ran for help with a yelp.	 ◯ The kelp stops the man from getting help.

1   Strap the clump of grass to the gate with your belt.

2   The tramp held on to the lamp post.

3   Tom had a gift of a damp tent made from soft silk.

4   The elk smelt of roses and milk.

5   Shall we skip and jump as we drift into the tent?

Handwriting – copy neatly.

mp

ft

lk

ct

Circle the odd one out. <u>Underline</u> the same.

<u>belt</u>	(bulk)	<u>felt</u>
lamp	damp	left
soft	text	loft
held	weld	bulb
raft	pact	tact
silk	strict	milk
elf	help	yelp
shelf	elf	left
lump	stump	pulp
lift	kilt	hilt

1   In the _____________ there was a small

_____________.

2   _____________ is a drink.

3   An attic is the name for a big _____________.

4   A _____________ can be
made from plastic.

5   The _____________ will _____________
on the tide.

6   Stan had a _____________
in his leg.

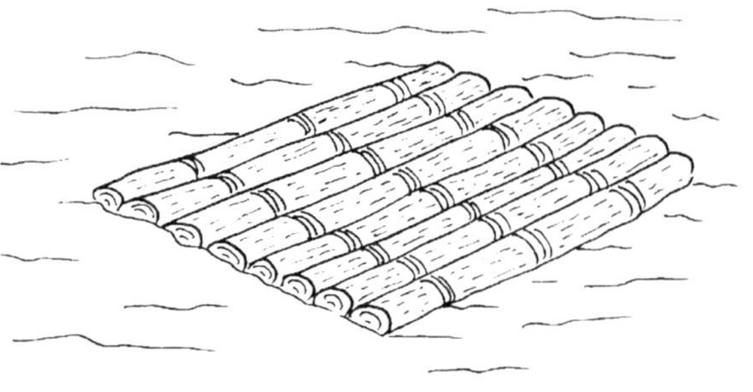

Use these words to complete the sentences.

raft	camp	lamp	drift
loft	belt	Milk	cramp

Wordsearch

p	a	c	t	d	g	i	f	t	t
u	g	w	u	h	e	l	d	y	i
m	a	u	q	e	l	c	a	n	p
p	p	s	l	l	f	k	m	e	g
j	c	a	m	p	b	g	p	x	r
l	l	h	e	s	b	e	l	t	t
j	o	c	l	a	m	p	a	e	m
w	f	b	t	f	h	u	c	l	l
s	t	u	f	t	i	l	t	k	e
k	g	d	a	o	r	p	e	y	f
m	b	f	d	l	c	s	x	p	t

Find these words.

pulp	lamp	melt	lob	tuft	loft
next	pact	gift	pump	camp	held
belt	act	damp	left	gulp	help

Lesson 10

My name is:

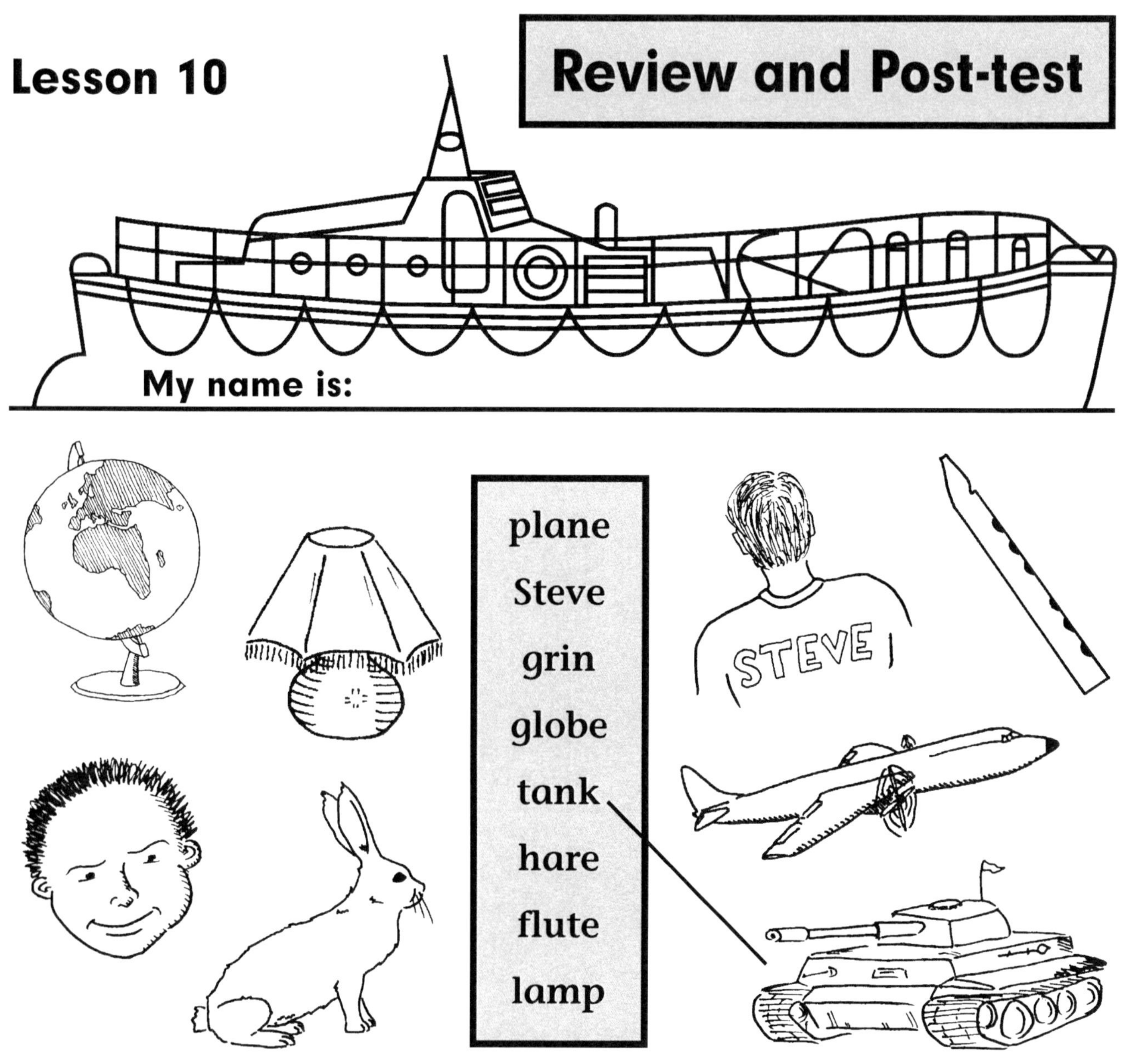

Track: *are, mp.*

bump	bare	rose	care	grab	flare
tank	limp	scare	fire	bang	camp
grin	Steve	jump	stare	wink	span
hose	spire	limp	bone	amp	hire
bunk	cone	hare	lung	share	wing
snare	stamp	grass	lamp	snore	graze
damp	wire	glare	cube	flames	wig

Word Match

Circle the same word.

1	**swim**	swine	swing	swum	(swim)
2	**milk**	elk	milk	silk	belt
3	**smoke**	mole	smile	smoke	rode
4	**plume**	plume	plum	plan	fumes
5	**score**	scare	score	more	store
6	**wing**	win	wink	swing	wing
7	**slope**	spoke	scope	slop	slope
8	**cake**	bake	cake	lake	snack

Spell and Write

Circle the letters. Write the word.

1	t ire	c ore	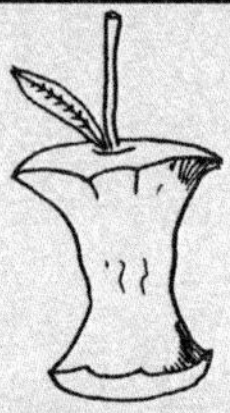	core
2	pl a ng	sl i nk	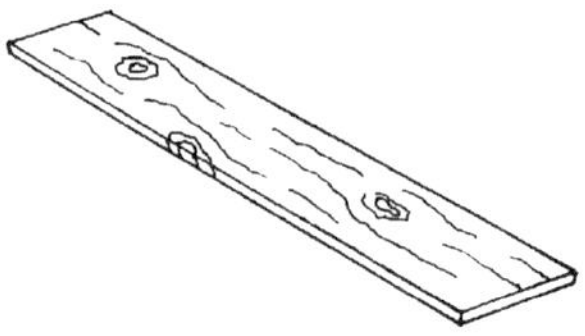	
3	m a ke	r o be	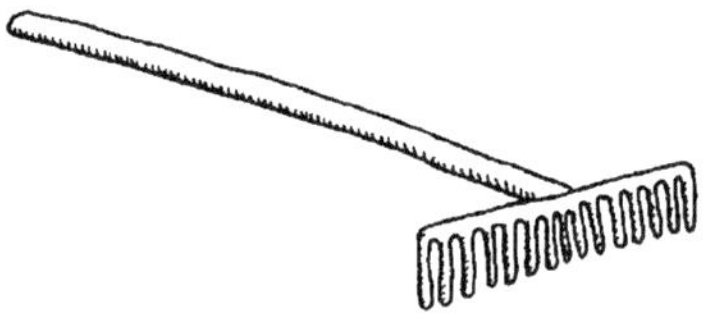	
4	cr u ke	dr a t	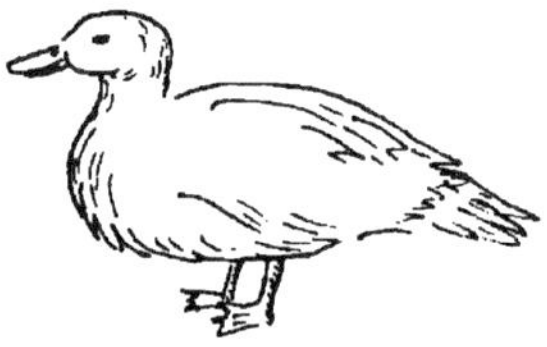	
5	l a ft	p i ct	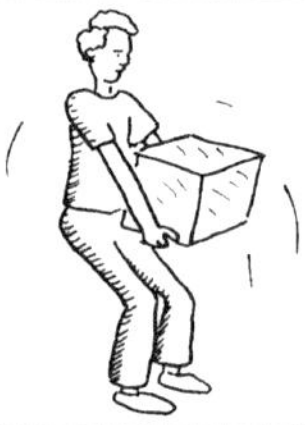	
6	f are	bl ire	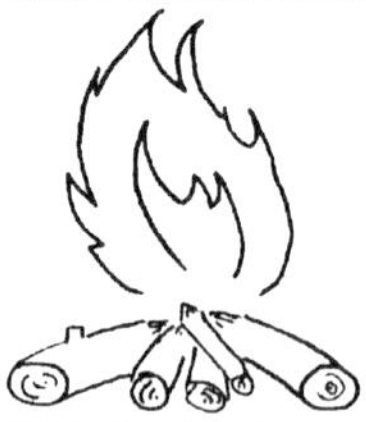	
7	c i te	k u be	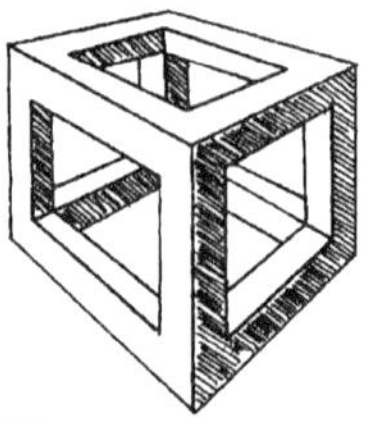	
8	c u mp	j e ft	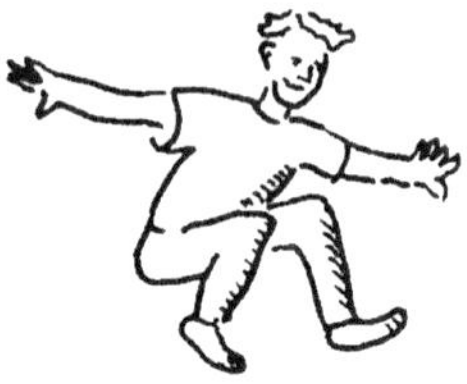	

1	✓ The Scot flaps at the smoke.	○ The Scot felt the smoke on his skin.
2	○ This snake helps Sandy.	○ This elk has a snack.
3	○ Billy will fill the milk jug.	○ Fill the jug up to the brim.
4	○ Tick tock went the clock.	○ The clock broke and spoke no more.
5	○ A stampede of elks.	○ The elks graze on the grass.
6	○ Glass bulbs can glare.	○ This bulb is plastic and bends.
7	○ The hill top is bare.	○ Glen's tank rolls up the hill.

1   The flag will flap in strong wind.

2   Andy can yell, skip and swim.

3   Lift the flute off the drum.

4   Flames from the fire stop the stampede.

5   If we stare at the elk it will be brave.

Handwriting – copy neatly.

nk

ore

mp

ft

Circle the odd one out. Underline the same.

1	<u>brake</u>	(spoke)	<u>snake</u>
2	Steve	Eve	have
3	bike	glide	slide
4	spire	fine	fire
5	tune	cube	tube
6	swim	slim	skip
7	fact	snack	pact
8	frost	pest	lost
9	bring	tank	bank
10	sore	wore	wire

1 _______________ fell from the sky.

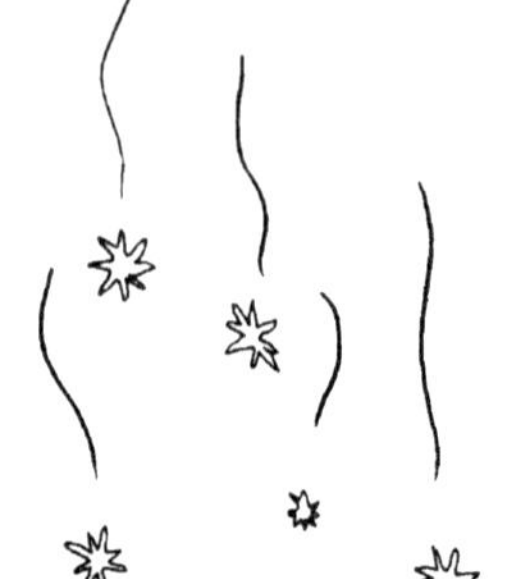

2 _______________ and _______________ smile
at the end of the tape.

3 The _______________ flops in the long grass.

4 Red _______________ are the best plants on the slope.

5 Luke sang a lovely _______________
to his grandad.

6 Wink and grin as the _______________ steps past.

7 Ron _______________ his tank
onto the raft.

Use these words to complete the sentences.

Steve	tune	Eve	rode
Flakes	frog	king	roses

Wordsearch

a	s	r	f	e	t	u	k	p	g
f	s	m	i	l	e	w	n	m	g
h	k	p	u	n	a	d	h	k	l
q	i	d	a	l	g	m	w	h	o
r	n	l	s	d	e	g	e	y	b
o	t	b	t	h	e	s	e	s	e
s	w	c	o	f	i	s	b	m	k
r	c	a	r	e	d	r	i	n	k
f	y	c	e	s	h	k	e	d	n
q	v	t	e	g	b	m	k	p	e
f	a	v	u	m	t	d	q	j	l

Find these words.

globe	spade	these	flames	mule
ring	drink	hire	care	store
smile	skin	act	hilt	side

Answers to Lesson 1

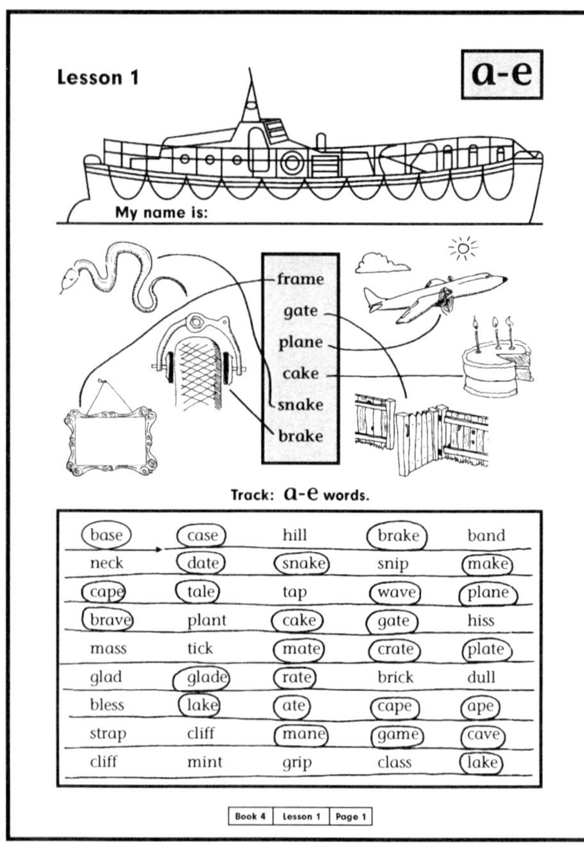

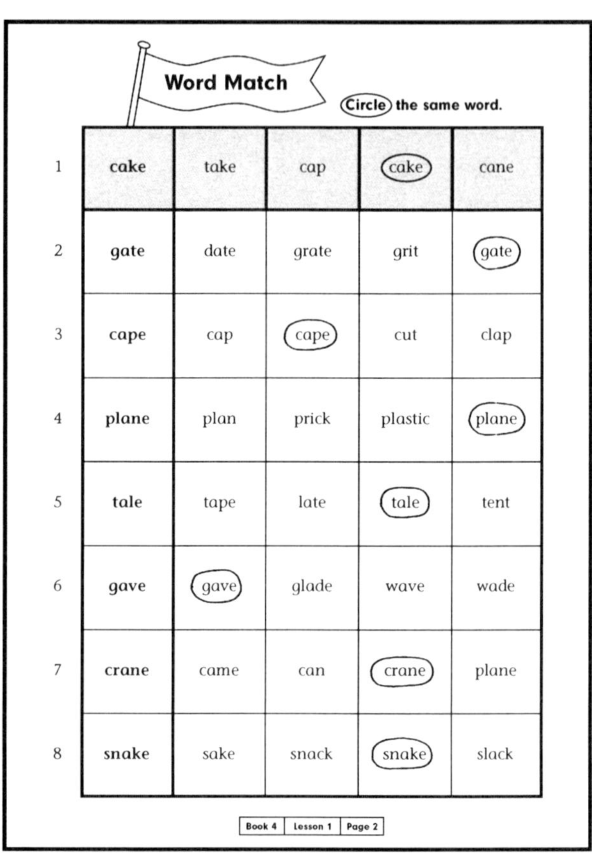

1	cake	take	cap	cake	cane
2	gate	date	grate	grit	gate
3	cape	cap	cape	cut	clap
4	plane	plan	prick	plastic	plane
5	tale	tape	late	tale	tent
6	gave	gave	glade	wave	wade
7	crane	came	can	crane	plane
8	snake	sake	snack	snake	slack

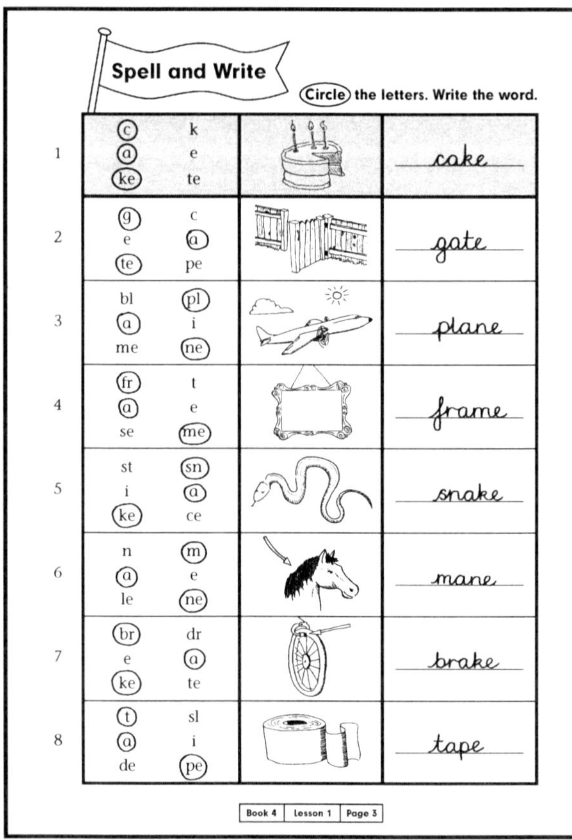

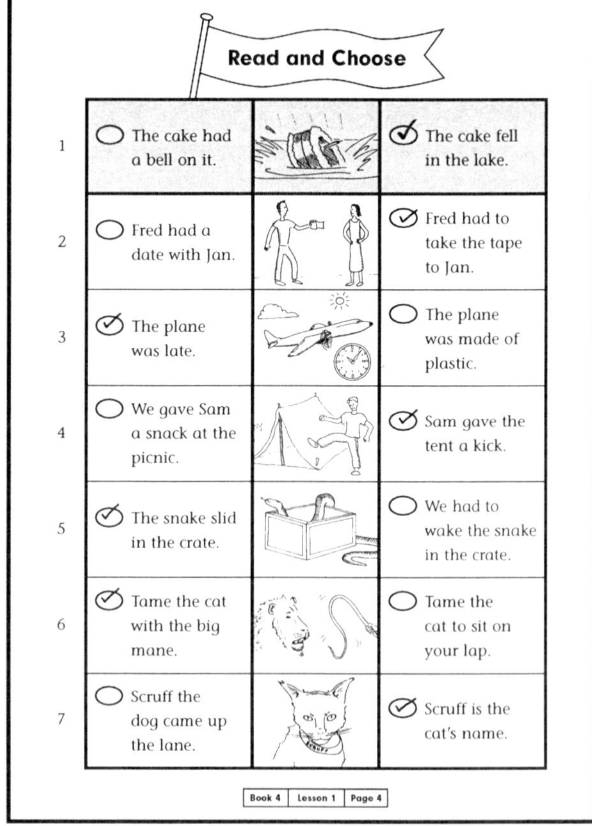

Dictation or Look – Say – Cover – Write – Check

1 Fred had a date with Scruff the dog.

Fred had a date with Scruff the dog.

2 The crab gave a wave to his mate.

The crab gave a wave to his mate.

3 The kite had a red strand made of plastic.

The kite had a red strand made of plastic.

4 Cross the lake to get to the gate.

Cross the lake to get to the gate.

5 Snuff the dog made a kid late for a date.

Snuff the dog made a kid late for a date.

Handwriting – copy neatly.

ate ate ate ate

lake lake lake lake

game game game game

brave brave brave brave

Listening Skills

Circle the odd one out. Underline the same.

1	make	cake	cape
2	date	take	rate
3	game	same	cane
4	made	mate	glade
5	crate	plane	lane
6	blade	wade	blame
7	crane	cape	cane
8	fade	spade	tale
9	lane	lame	dame
10	plane	Jane	fame

Cloze Procedure

1 Ben can make a cake in the tin.

2 Sam had a date with Kim.

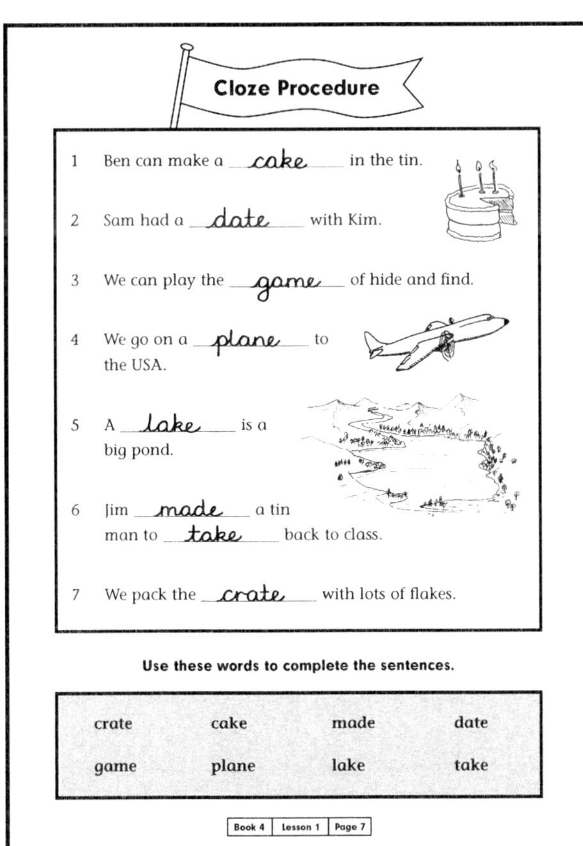

3 We can play the game of hide and find.

4 We go on a plane to the USA.

5 A lake is a big pond.

6 Jim made a tin man to take back to class.

7 We pack the crate with lots of flakes.

Use these words to complete the sentences.

crate	cake	made	date
game	plane	lake	take

Wordsearch

q	t	e	r	u	m	t	o	g	r
f	a	d	b	r	a	k	e	l	k
a	p	e	s	n	k	c	x	a	x
k	e	g	m	h	e	p	b	d	g
e	c	f	c	a	v	e	h	e	h
x	m	a	a	t	e	g	x	d	l
b	n	a	p	e	n	g	a	g	a
n	z	f	v	e	b	p	s	m	k
c	a	m	e	x	h	t	a	m	e
h	d	a	t	e	t	a	l	e	f
f	z	a	g	b	w	v	e	n	m

Find these words.

ape	ate	brake	came	cape	cave
date	game	glade	hate	sale	tame
tape	tale	lake	nape	make	fake

Answers to Lesson 2

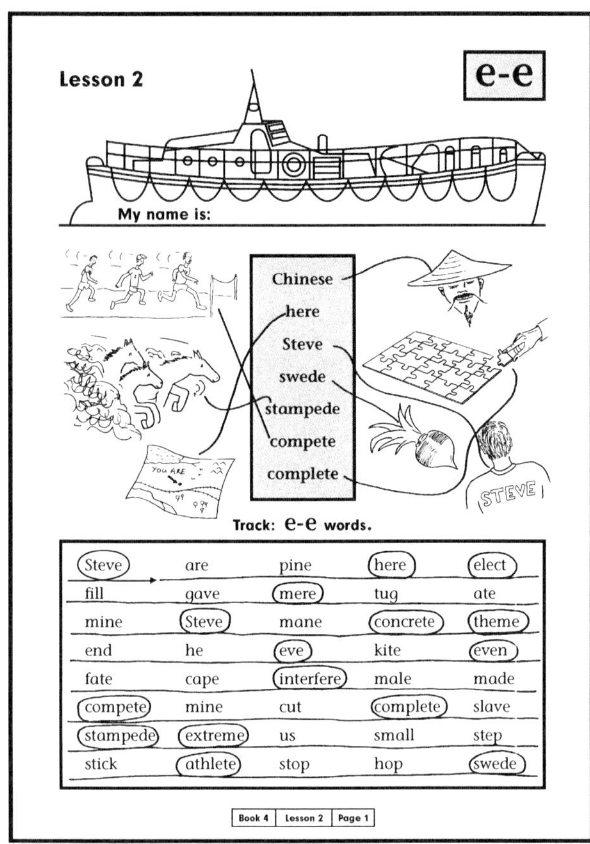

(Steve)	are	pine	(here)	(elect)
fill	gave	(mere)	tug	ate
mine	(Steve)	mane	(concrete)	(theme)
end	he	(eve)	kite	(even)
fate	cape	(interfere)	male	made
(compete)	mine	cut	(complete)	slave
(stampede)	(extreme)	us	small	step
stick	(athlete)	stop	hop	(swede)

Book 4 | Lesson 2 | Page 1

1	compete	compare	complete	(compete)	Pete
2	here	hot	rest	her	(here)
3	these	their	(these)	his	hem
4	eve	vent	even	here	(eve)
5	Steve	Steven	stop	(Steve)	step
6	swede	(swede)	wed	west	sand
7	complete	compete	plate	(complete)	comic
8	mere	here	(mere)	Eve	mine

Book 4 | Lesson 2 | Page 2

	Letters	Picture	Word
1	(h) f / a (e) / (re) me		*here*
2	(Chi) th / i (ne) / (se) te		*Chinese*
3	con (com) / a (pe) / (te) re		*compete*
4	(stam) sted / a (pe) / (de) te		*stampede*
5	(con) cos / (cre) a / de (te)		*concrete*
6	sh (sw) / (e) a / (de) te		*swede*
7	(E) n / e (v) / te (e)		*Eve*
8	th (com) / e (ple) / (te) me		*complete*

Book 4 | Lesson 2 | Page 3

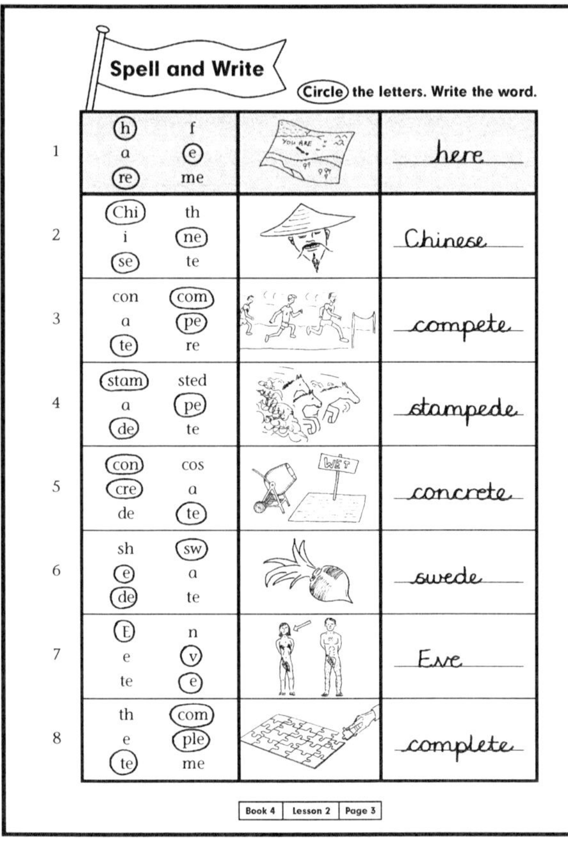

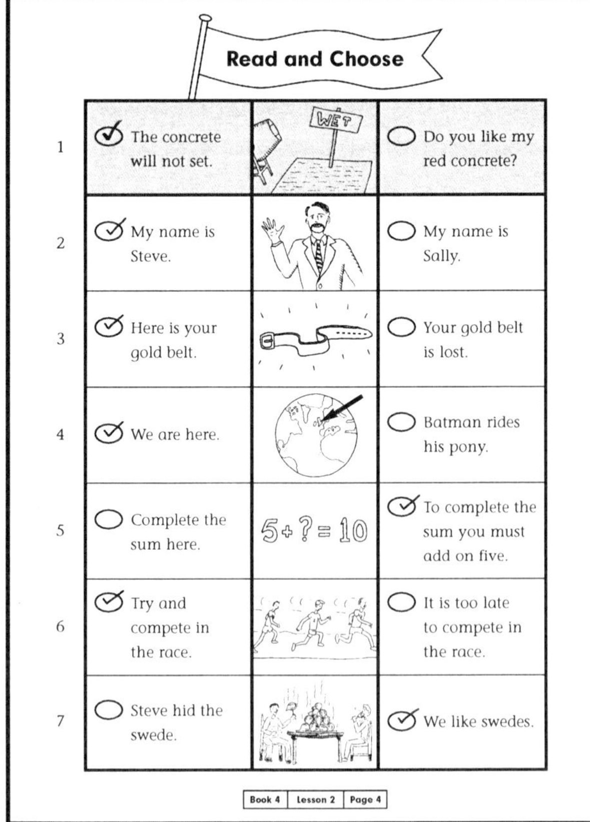

1	☑ The concrete will not set.	WET	○ Do you like my red concrete?
2	☑ My name is Steve.		○ My name is Sally.
3	☑ Here is your gold belt.		○ Your gold belt is lost.
4	☑ We are here.		○ Batman rides his pony.
5	○ Complete the sum here.	$5 + ? = 10$	☑ To complete the sum you must add on five.
6	☑ Try and compete in the race.		○ It is too late to compete in the race.
7	○ Steve hid the swede.		☑ We like swedes.

Book 4 | Lesson 2 | Page 4

94

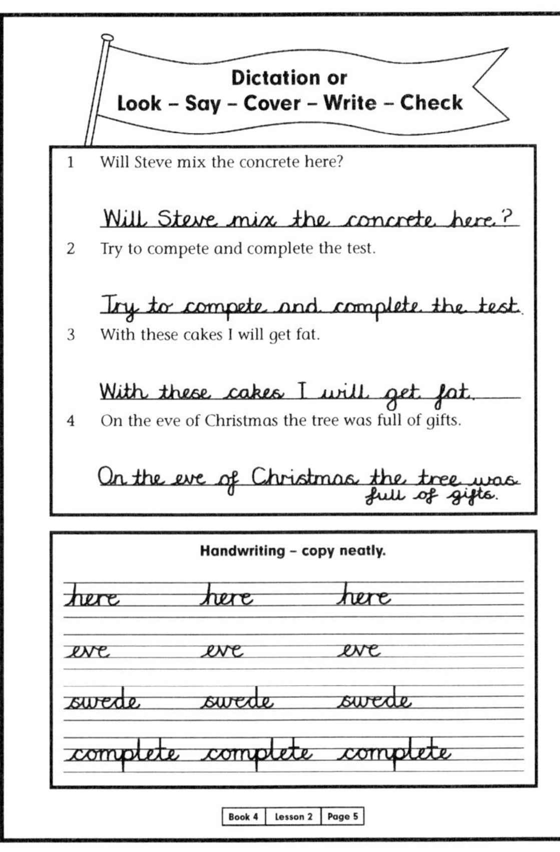

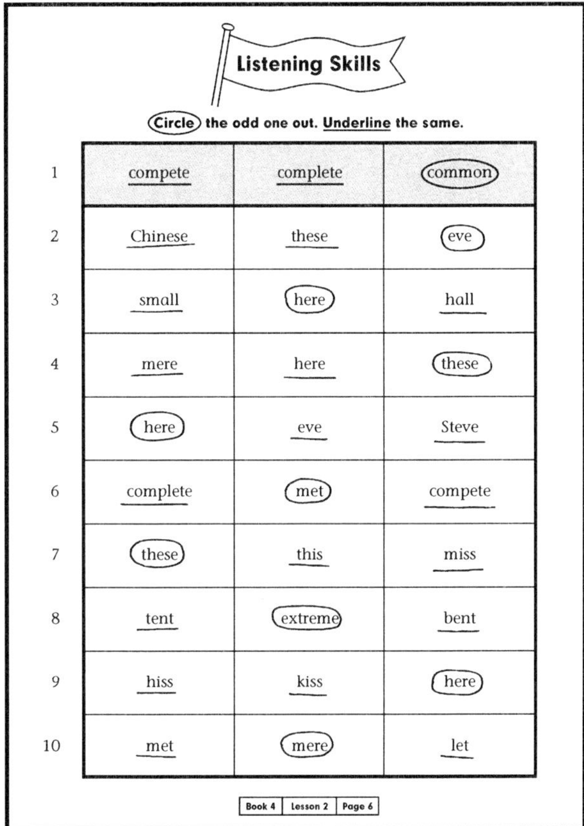

1	compete	complete	(common)
2	Chinese	these	(eve)
3	small	(here)	hall
4	mere	here	(these)
5	(here)	eve	Steve
6	complete	(met)	compete
7	(these)	this	miss
8	tent	(extreme)	bent
9	hiss	kiss	(here)
10	met	(mere)	let

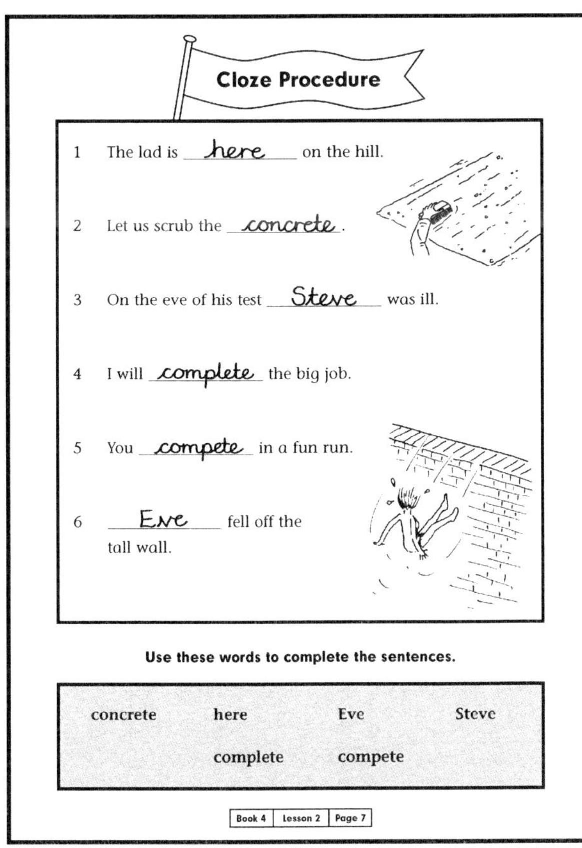

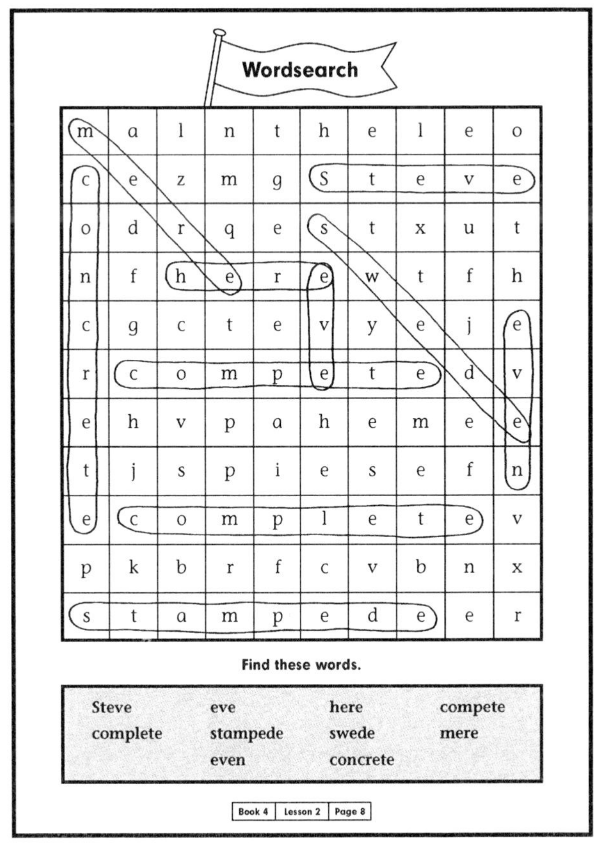

m	a	l	n	t	h	e	l	e	o
c	e	z	m	g	S	t	e	v	e
o	d	r	q	e	s	t	x	u	t
n	f	h	e	r	e	w	t	f	h
c	g	c	t	e	v	y	e	j	e
r	c	o	m	p	e	t	e	d	v
e	h	v	p	a	h	e	m	e	e
t	j	s	p	i	e	s	e	f	n
e	c	o	m	p	l	e	t	e	v
p	k	b	r	f	c	v	b	n	x
s	t	a	m	p	e	d	e	e	r

Answers to Lesson 3

flog	grab	black	slap	glad	slug	frost
flab	pram	snap	frill	spin	glint	grill
drag	fled	plum	from	plan	flit	trap
grass	drip	glum	clan	flack	nest	grant
clap	flock	stub	grand	stun	frog	fist
glide	mist	tram	flip	slap	trip	grip
grit	slug	flint	dust	glass	stop	fret
drat	gram	stun	frantic	bred	flick	snug
grim	fly	flat	glade	rest	frock	slop
grasp	best	land	mint	flap	from	gran

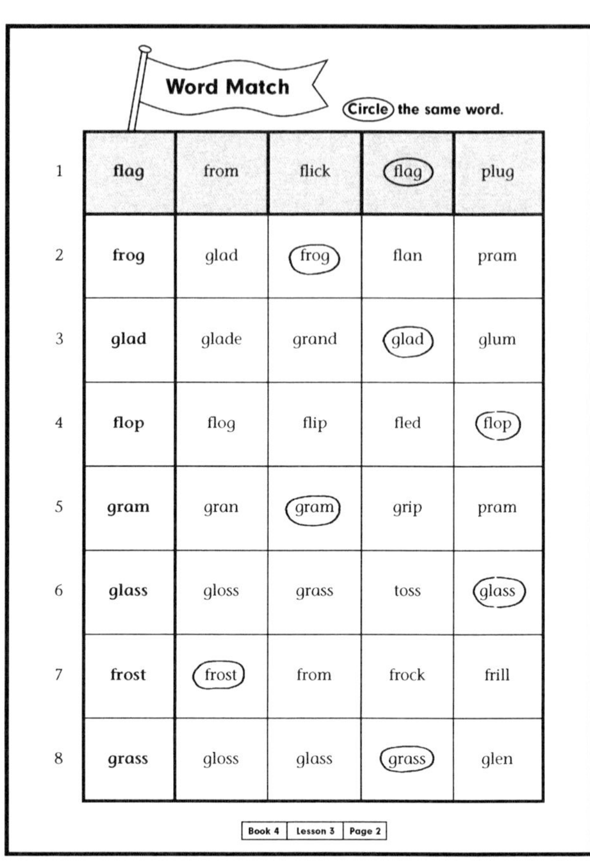

Word Match

Circle the same word.

1	flag	from	flick	**flag**	plug
2	frog	glad	**frog**	flan	pram
3	glad	glade	grand	**glad**	glum
4	flop	flog	flip	fled	**flop**
5	gram	gran	**gram**	grip	pram
6	glass	gloss	grass	toss	**glass**
7	frost	**frost**	from	frock	frill
8	grass	gloss	glass	**grass**	glen

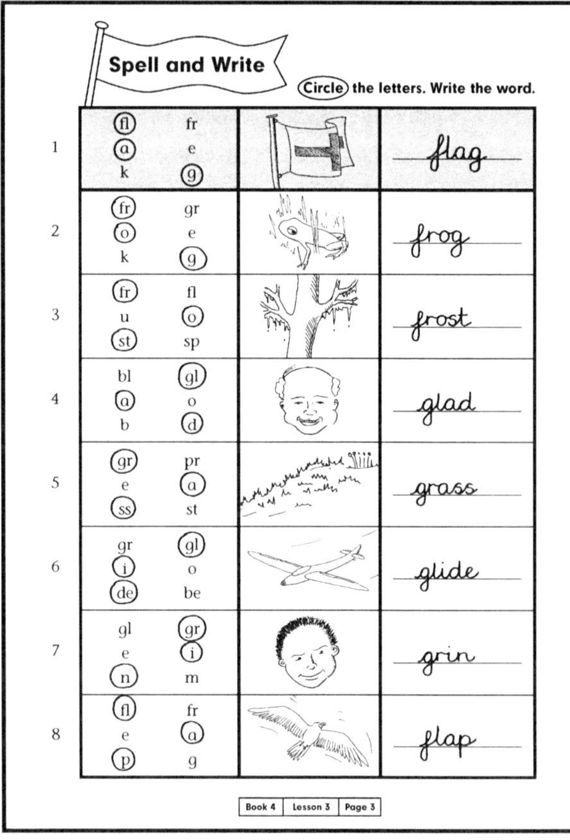

Spell and Write

Circle the letters. Write the word.

1	**fl** a k	fr e **g**		*flag*
2	**fr** **o** k	gr e **g**		*frog*
3	**fr** u **st**	fl **o** sp		*frost*
4	bl **a** b	**gl** o **d**		*glad*
5	**gr** e **ss**	pr **a** st		*grass*
6	gr **i** **de**	**gl** o be		*glide*
7	gl e **n**	**gr** **i** m		*grin*
8	**fl** e **p**	fr **a** g		*flap*

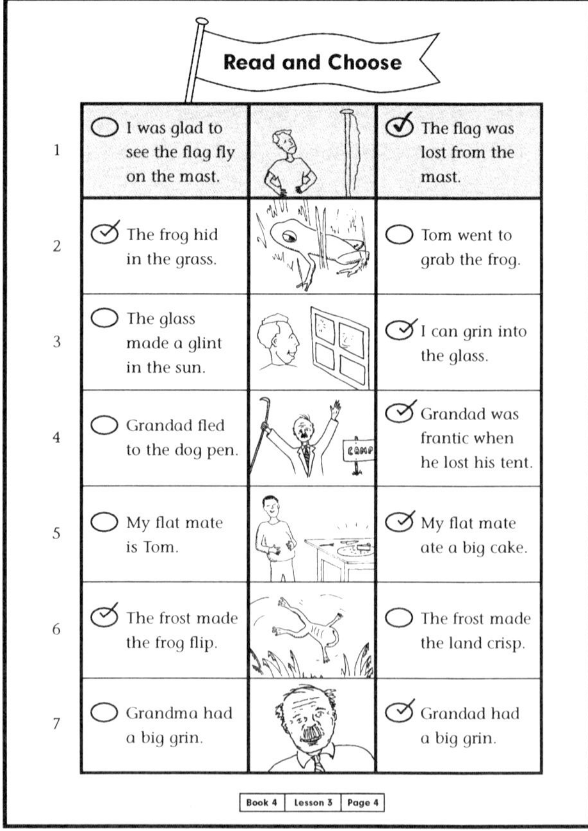

Read and Choose

1	○ I was glad to see the flag fly on the mast.		✓ The flag was lost from the mast.
2	✓ The frog hid in the grass.		○ Tom went to grab the frog.
3	○ The glass made a glint in the sun.		✓ I can grin into the glass.
4	○ Grandad fled to the dog pen.		✓ Grandad was frantic when he lost his tent.
5	○ My flat mate is Tom.		✓ My flat mate ate a big cake.
6	✓ The frost made the frog flip.		○ The frost made the land crisp.
7	○ Grandma had a big grin.		✓ Grandad had a big grin.

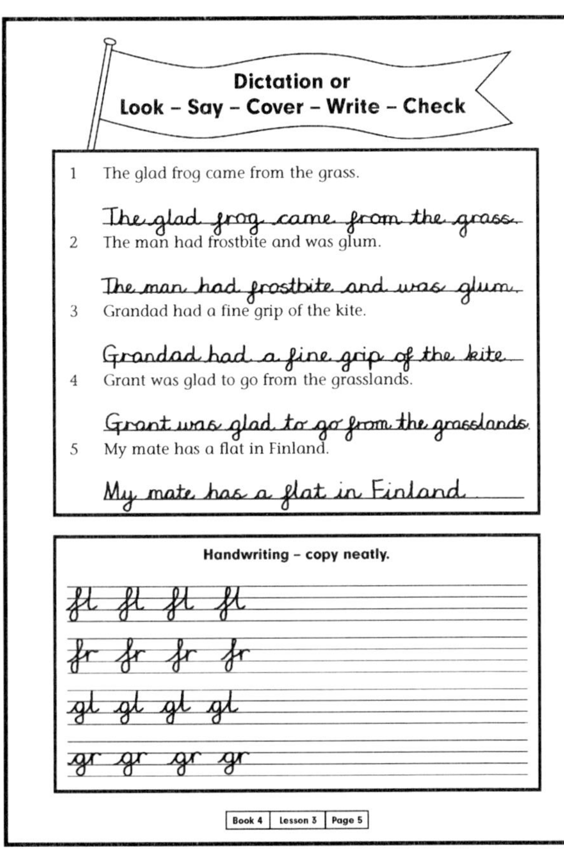

Dictation or Look – Say – Cover – Write – Check

1 The glad frog came from the grass.

The glad frog came from the grass.

2 The man had frostbite and was glum.

The man had frostbite and was glum.

3 Grandad had a fine grip of the kite.

Grandad had a fine grip of the kite

4 Grant was glad to go from the grasslands.

Grant was glad to go from the grasslands.

5 My mate has a flat in Finland.

My mate has a flat in Finland

Handwriting – copy neatly.

fl fl fl fl

fr fr fr fr

gl gl gl gl

gr gr gr gr

Book 4 | Lesson 3 | Page 5

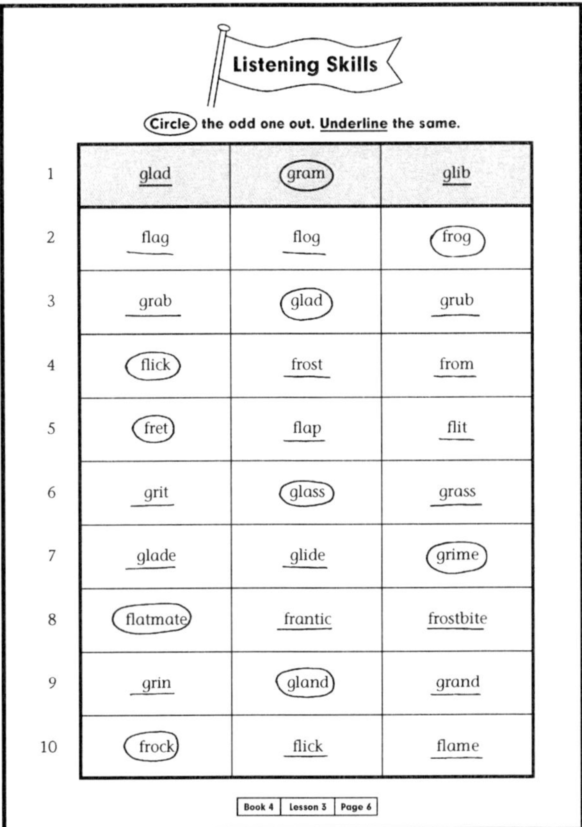

Listening Skills

Circle the odd one out. Underline the same.

1	glad	gram	glib
2	flag	flog	frog
3	grab	glad	grub
4	flick	frost	from
5	fret	flap	flit
6	grit	glass	grass
7	glade	glide	grime
8	flatmate	frantic	frostbite
9	grin	gland	grand
10	frock	flick	flame

Book 4 | Lesson 3 | Page 6

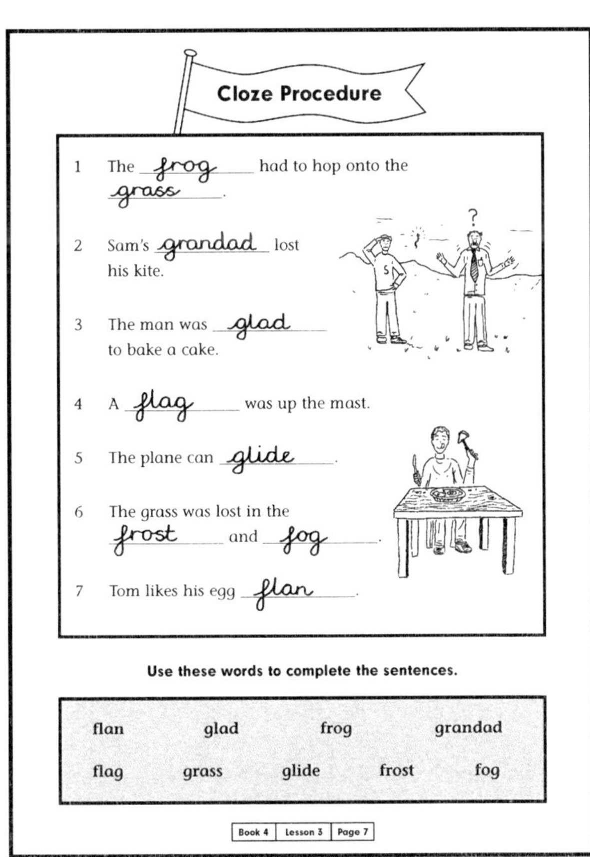

Cloze Procedure

1 The _frog_ had to hop onto the _grass_ .

2 Sam's _grandad_ lost his kite.

3 The man was _glad_ to bake a cake.

4 A _flag_ was up the mast.

5 The plane can _glide_ .

6 The grass was lost in the _frost_ and _fog_ .

7 Tom likes his egg _flan_ .

Use these words to complete the sentences.

flan	glad	frog	grandad
flag	grass	glide	frost	fog

Book 4 | Lesson 3 | Page 7

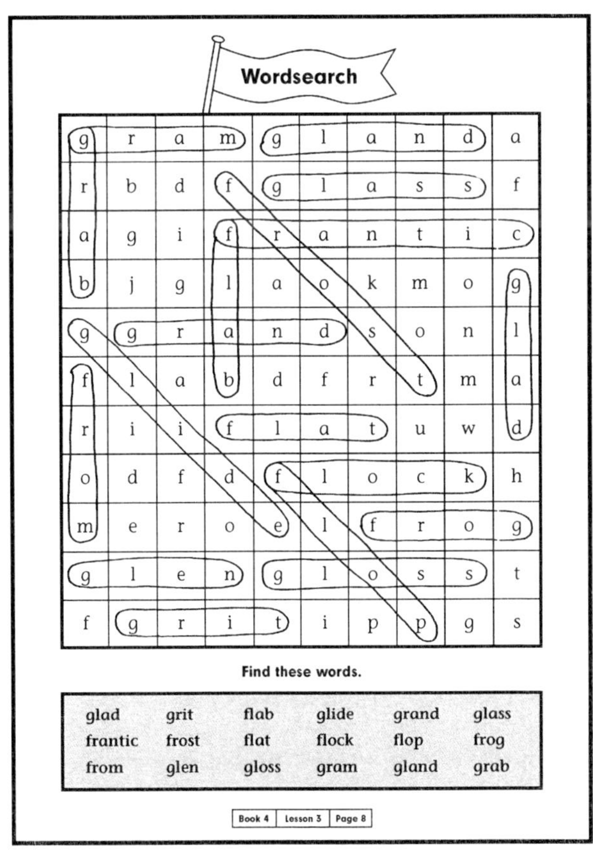

Wordsearch

g	r	a	m	g	l	a	n	d	a
r	b	d	f	g	l	a	s	s	f
a	g	i	f	r	a	n	t	i	c
b	j	g	l	a	o	k	m	o	g
g	g	r	a	n	d	s	o	n	l
f	l	a	b	d	f	r	t	m	a
r	i	i	f	l	a	t	u	w	d
o	d	f	f	l	o	c	k	h
m	e	r	o	e	l	f	r	o	g
g	l	e	n	g	l	o	s	s	t
f	g	r	i	t	i	p	p	g	s

Find these words.

glad	grit	flab	glide	grand	glass
frantic	frost	flat	flock	flop	frog
from	glen	gloss	gram	gland	grab

Book 4 | Lesson 3 | Page 8

Answers to Lesson 4

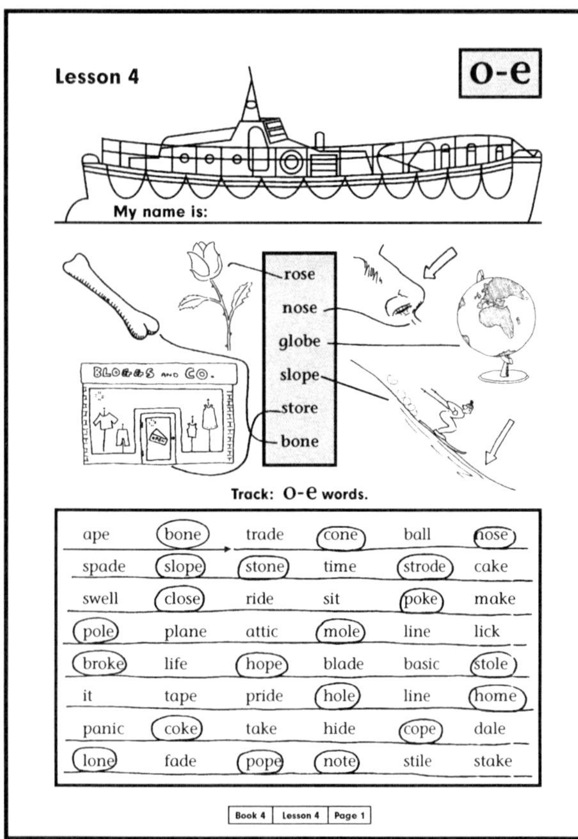

Lesson 4 — Page 1 (Track: o-e words)

ape	(bone)	trade	(cone)	ball	(nose)
spade	(slope)	(stone)	time	(strode)	cake
swell	(close)	ride	sit	(poke)	make
(pole)	plane	attic	(mole)	line	lick
(broke)	life	(hope)	blade	basic	(stole)
it	tape	pride	(hole)	line	(home)
panic	(coke)	take	hide	(cope)	dale
(lone)	fade	(pope)	(note)	stile	stake

Book 4 | Lesson 4 | Page 1

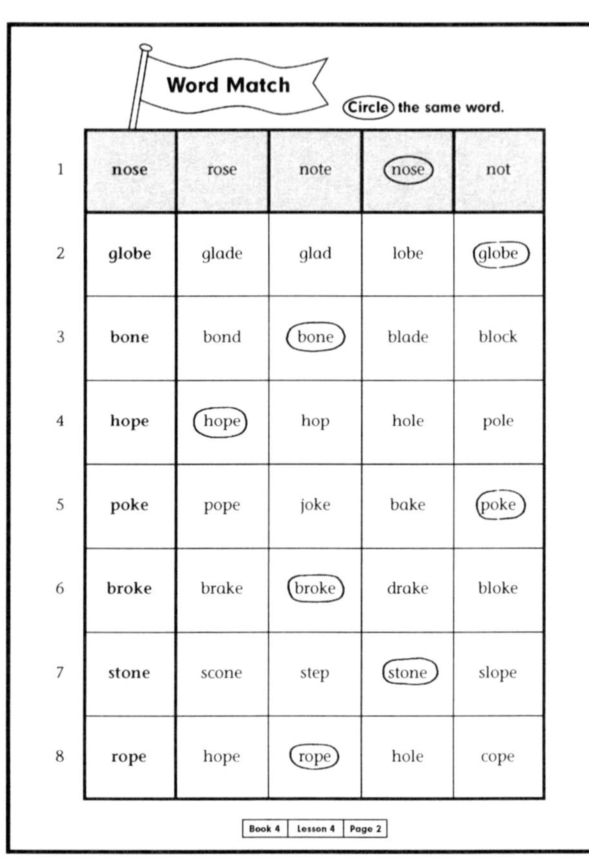

Word Match

1	nose	rose	note	(nose)	not
2	globe	glade	glad	lobe	(globe)
3	bone	bond	(bone)	blade	block
4	hope	(hope)	hop	hole	pole
5	poke	pope	joke	bake	(poke)
6	broke	brake	(broke)	drake	bloke
7	stone	scone	step	(stone)	slope
8	rope	hope	(rope)	hole	cope

Book 4 | Lesson 4 | Page 2

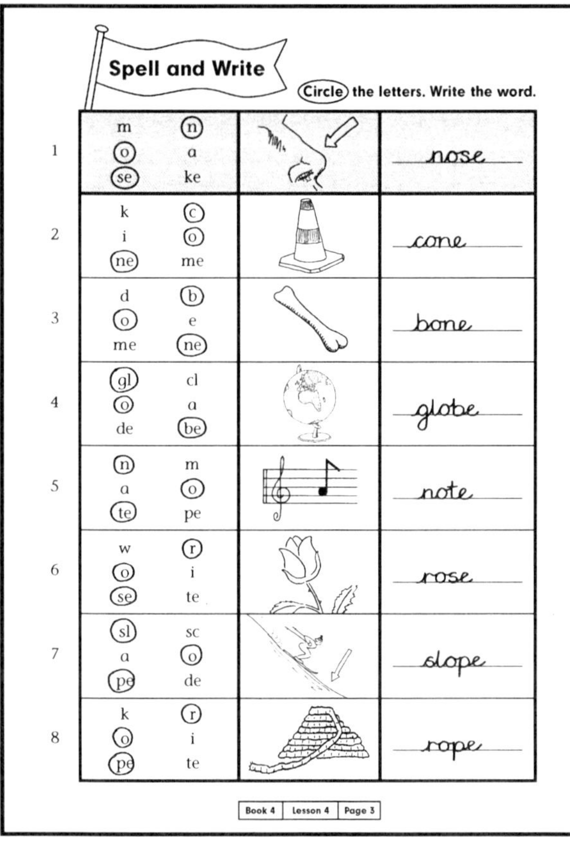

Spell and Write

	Letters		Word
1	m / (n) / (se)	a / ke	nose
2	k / i / (ne)	(c) / (o) / me	cone
3	d / (o) / me	(b) / e / (ne)	bone
4	(gl) / (o) / de	cl / a / (be)	globe
5	(n) / a / (te)	m / (o) / pe	note
6	w / (o) / (se)	(r) / i / te	rose
7	(sl) / a / (pe)	sc / (o) / de	slope
8	k / (o) / (pe)	(r) / i / te	rope

Book 4 | Lesson 4 | Page 3

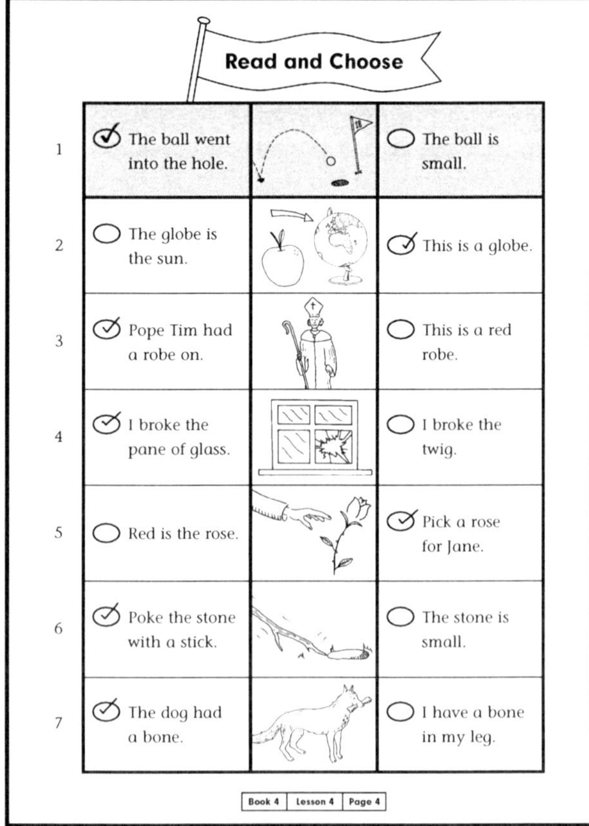

Read and Choose

1	✓ The ball went into the hole.		◯ The ball is small.
2	◯ The globe is the sun.		✓ This is a globe.
3	✓ Pope Tim had a robe on.		◯ This is a red robe.
4	✓ I broke the pane of glass.		◯ I broke the twig.
5	◯ Red is the rose.		✓ Pick a rose for Jane.
6	✓ Poke the stone with a stick.		◯ The stone is small.
7	✓ The dog had a bone.		◯ I have a bone in my leg.

Book 4 | Lesson 4 | Page 4

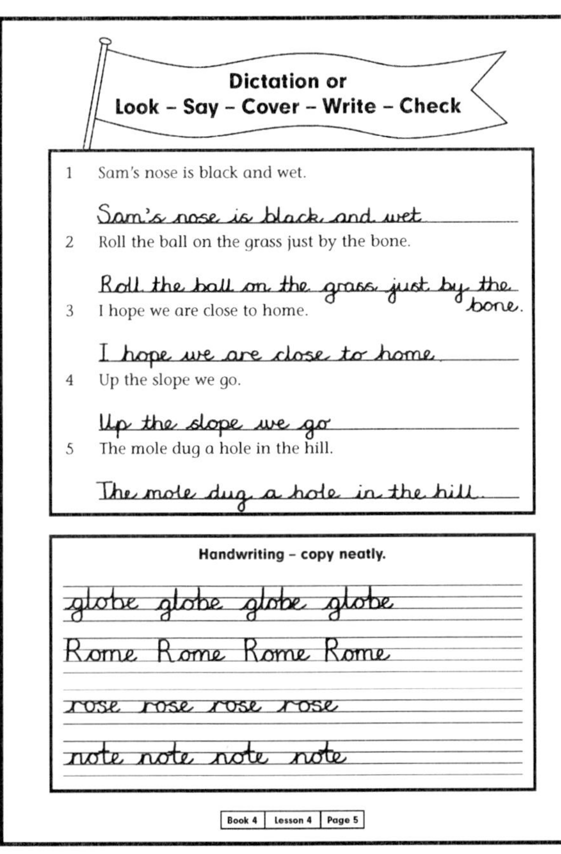

Dictation or Look – Say – Cover – Write – Check

1 Sam's nose is black and wet.

Sam's nose is black and wet

2 Roll the ball on the grass just by the bone.

Roll the ball on the grass just by the bone.

3 I hope we are close to home.

I hope we are close to home.

4 Up the slope we go.

Up the slope we go

5 The mole dug a hole in the hill.

The mole dug a hole in the hill.

Handwriting – copy neatly.

globe globe globe globe

Rome Rome Rome Rome

rose rose rose rose

note note note note

Book 4 | Lesson 4 | Page 5

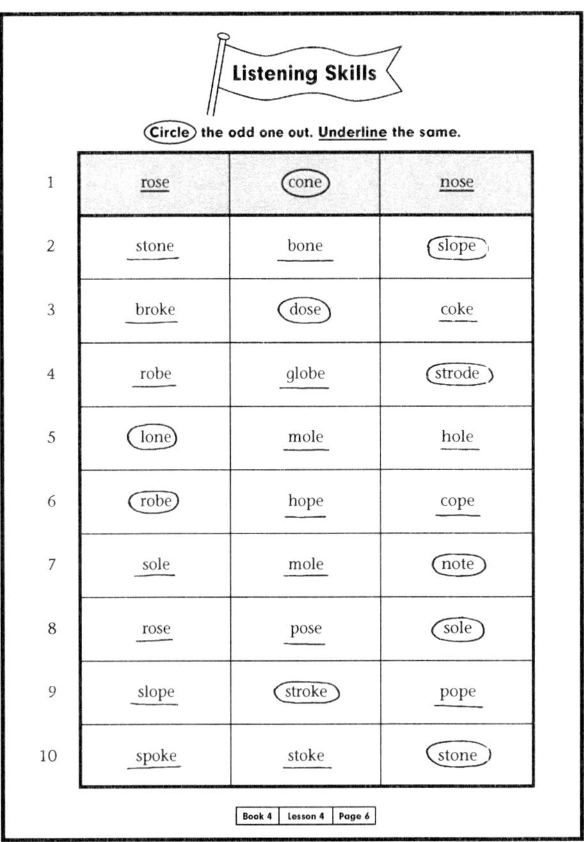

Listening Skills

(Circle) the odd one out. Underline the same.

1	rose	cone	nose
2	stone	bone	slope
3	broke	dose	coke
4	robe	globe	strode
5	lone	mole	hole
6	robe	hope	cope
7	sole	mole	note
8	rose	pose	sole
9	slope	stroke	pope
10	spoke	stoke	stone

Book 4 | Lesson 4 | Page 6

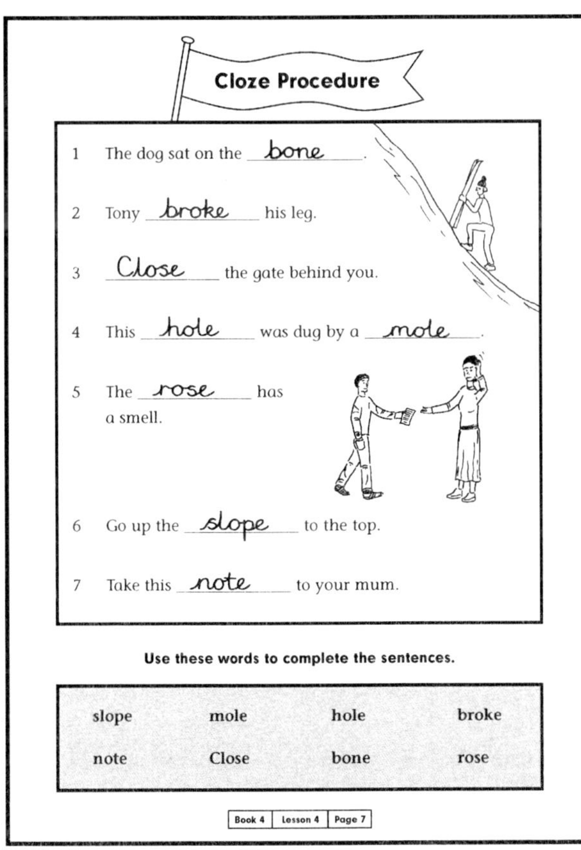

Cloze Procedure

1 The dog sat on the *bone*.

2 Tony *broke* his leg.

3 *Close* the gate behind you.

4 This *hole* was dug by a *mole*.

5 The *rose* has a smell.

6 Go up the *slope* to the top.

7 Take this *note* to your mum.

Use these words to complete the sentences.

slope	mole	hole	broke
note	Close	bone	rose

Book 4 | Lesson 4 | Page 7

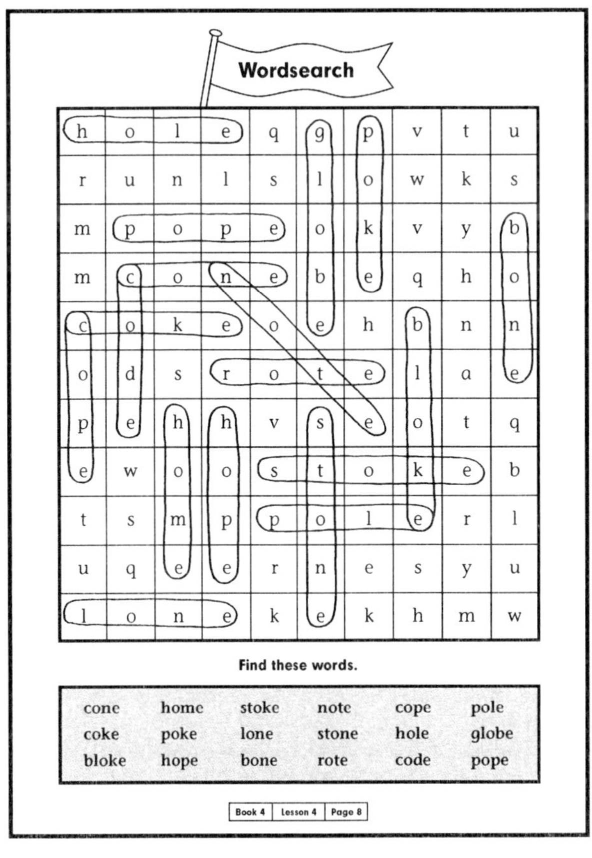

Wordsearch

h	o	l	e	q	g	p	v	t	u
r	u	n	l	s	l	o	w	k	s
m	p	o	p	e	o	k	v	y	b
m	c	o	n	e	b	e	q	h	o
c	o	k	e	o	e	h	b	n	n
o	d	s	r	o	t	e	l	a	e
p	e	h	h	v	s	e	o	t	q
e	w	o	o	s	t	o	k	e	b
t	s	m	p	p	o	l	e	r	l
u	q	e	e	r	n	e	s	y	u
l	o	n	e	k	e	k	h	m	w

Find these words.

cone	home	stoke	note	cope	pole
coke	poke	lone	stone	hole	globe
bloke	hope	bone	rote	code	pope

Book 4 | Lesson 4 | Page 8

99

Answers to Lesson 5

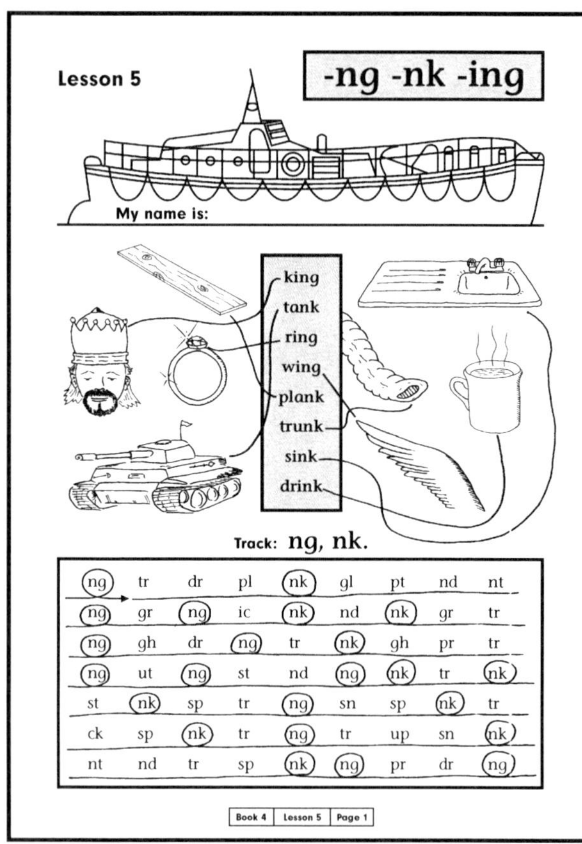

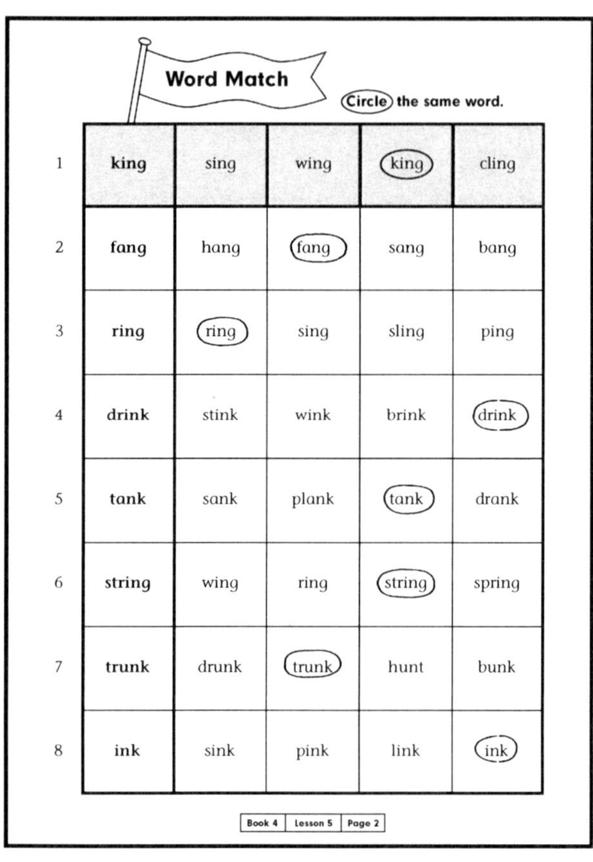

1	king	sing	wing	(king)	cling
2	fang	hang	(fang)	sang	bang
3	ring	(ring)	sing	sling	ping
4	drink	stink	wink	brink	(drink)
5	tank	sank	plank	(tank)	drank
6	string	wing	ring	(string)	spring
7	trunk	drunk	(trunk)	hunt	bunk
8	ink	sink	pink	link	(ink)

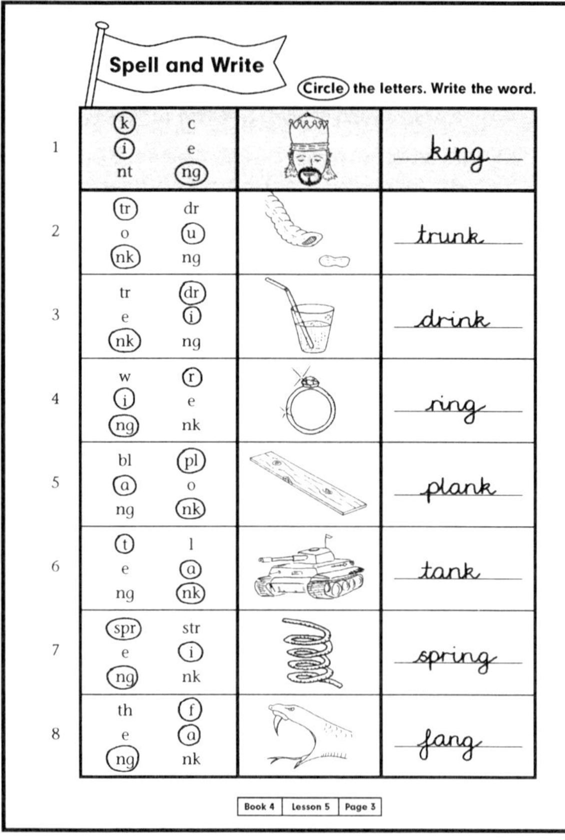

			Word
1	(k) c / (i) e / nt (ng)		king
2	(tr) dr / o (u) / (nk) ng		trunk
3	tr (dr) / e (i) / (nk) ng		drink
4	w (r) / (i) e / (ng) nk		ring
5	bl (pl) / (a) o / ng (nk)		plank
6	(t) l / e (a) / ng (nk)		tank
7	(spr) str / e (i) / (ng) nk		spring
8	th (f) / e (a) / (ng) nk		fang

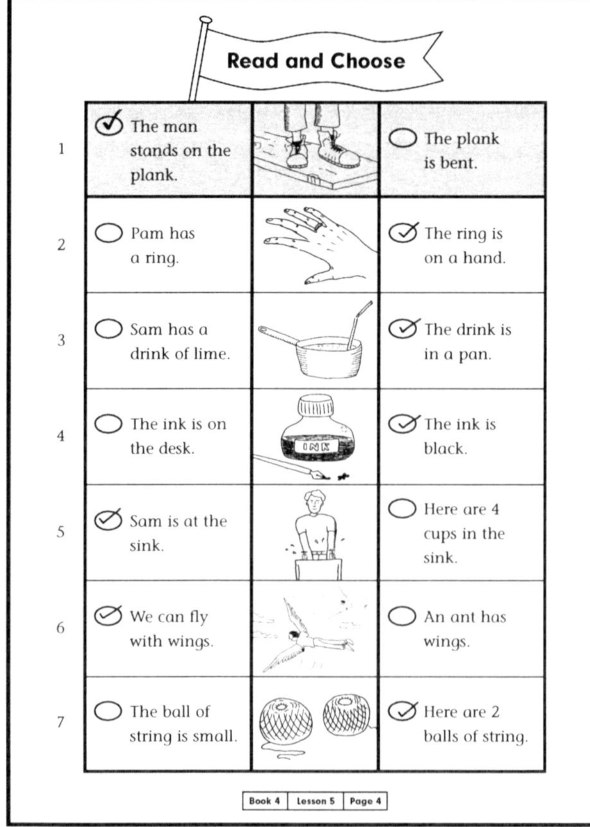

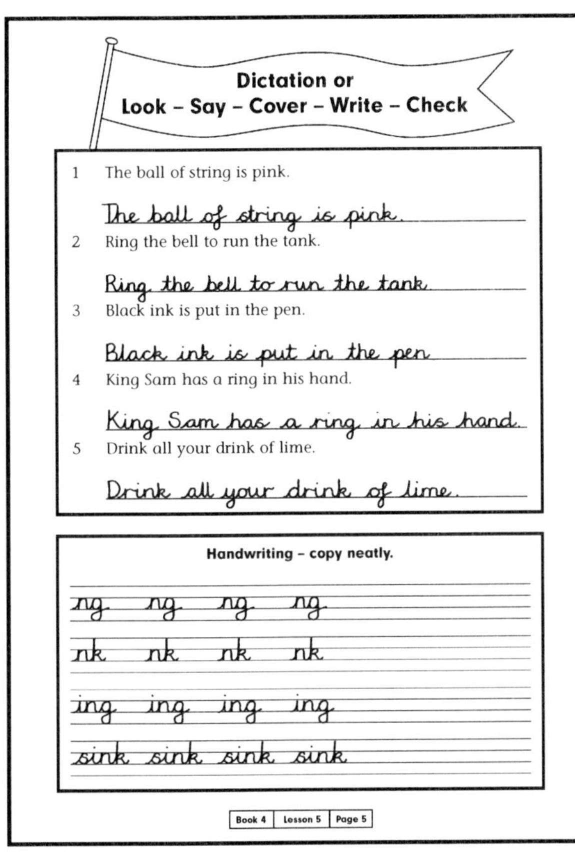

Dictation or Look – Say – Cover – Write – Check

1 The ball of string is pink.

The ball of string is pink.

2 Ring the bell to run the tank.

Ring the bell to run the tank

3 Black ink is put in the pen.

Black ink is put in the pen

4 King Sam has a ring in his hand.

King Sam has a ring in his hand.

5 Drink all your drink of lime.

Drink all your drink of lime.

Handwriting – copy neatly.

ng   ng   ng   ng

nk   nk   nk   nk

ing   ing   ing   ing

sink   sink   sink   sink

Book 4 | Lesson 5 | Page 5

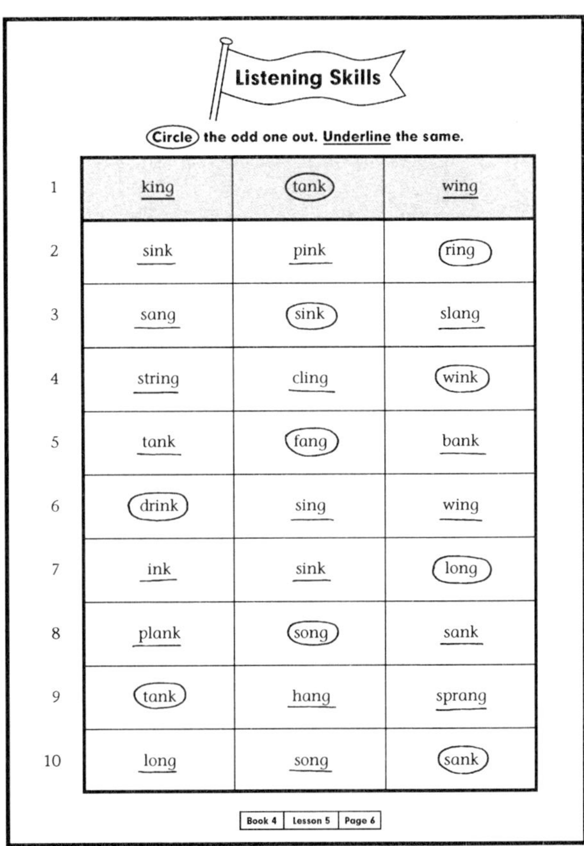

Listening Skills

Circle the odd one out. Underline the same.

1	king	tank	wing
2	sink	pink	ring
3	sang	sink	slang
4	string	cling	wink
5	tank	fang	bank
6	drink	sing	wing
7	ink	sink	long
8	plank	song	sank
9	tank	hang	sprang
10	long	song	sank

Book 4 | Lesson 5 | Page 6

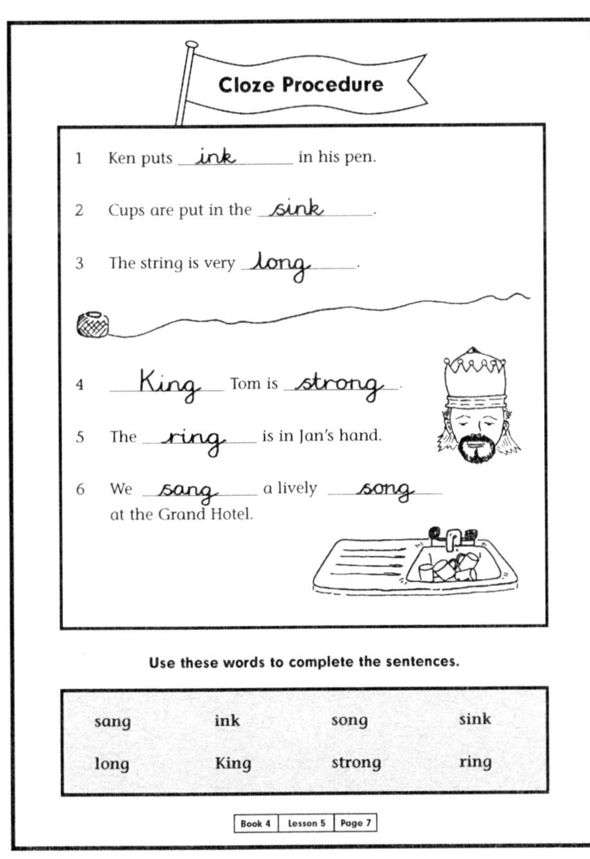

Cloze Procedure

1 Ken puts __ink__ in his pen.

2 Cups are put in the __sink__.

3 The string is very __long__

4 __King__ Tom is __strong__.

5 The __ring__ is in Jan's hand.

6 We __sang__ a lively __song__ at the Grand Hotel.

Use these words to complete the sentences.

sang	ink	song	sink
long	King	strong	ring

Book 4 | Lesson 5 | Page 7

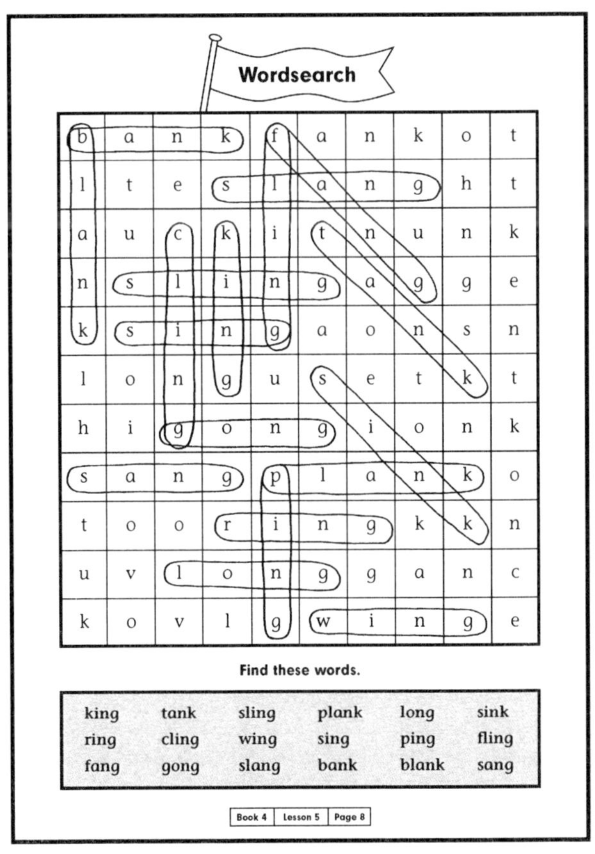

Wordsearch

b	a	n	k	f	a	n	k	o	t
l	t	e	s	l	a	n	g	h	t
a	u	c	k	i	t	n	u	n	k
n	s	l	i	n	g	a	g	g	e
k	s	i	n	g	a	o	n	s	n
l	o	n	g	u	s	e	t	k	t
h	i	g	o	n	g	i	o	n	k
s	a	n	g	p	l	a	n	k	o
t	o	o	r	i	n	g	k	k	n
u	v	l	o	n	g	g	a	n	c
k	o	v	l	g	w	i	n	g	e

Find these words.

king	tank	sling	plank	long	sink
ring	cling	wing	sing	ping	fling
fang	gong	slang	bank	blank	sang

Book 4 | Lesson 5 | Page 8

Answers to Lesson 6

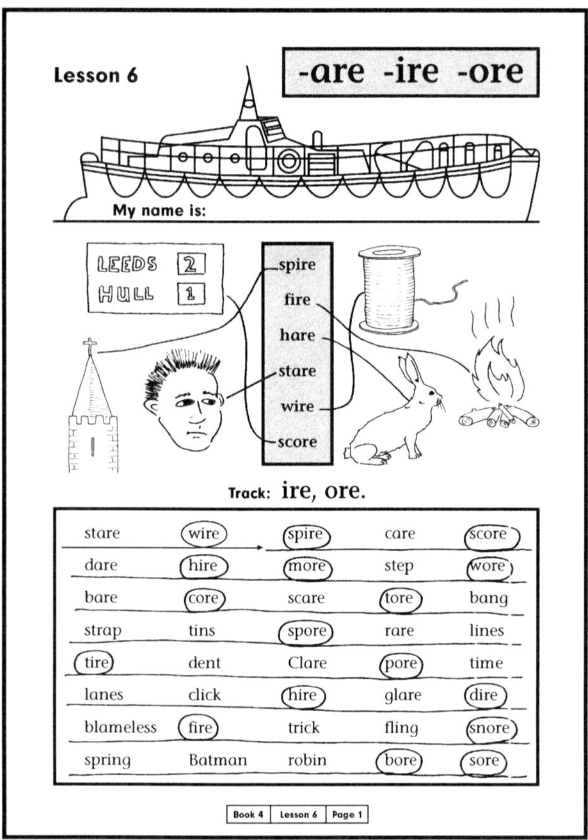

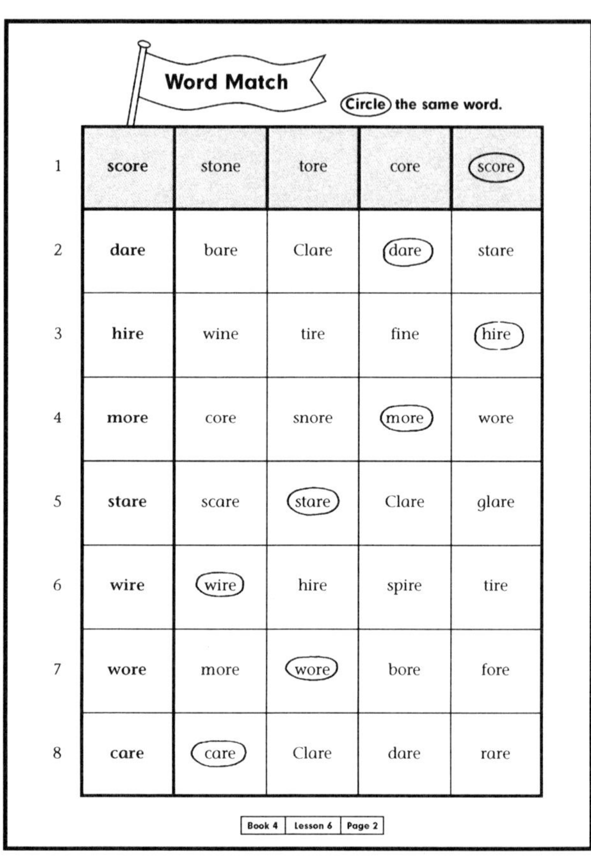

#					
1	score	stone	tore	core	(score)
2	dare	bare	Clare	(dare)	stare
3	hire	wine	tire	fine	(hire)
4	more	core	snore	(more)	wore
5	stare	scare	(stare)	Clare	glare
6	wire	(wire)	hire	spire	tire
7	wore	more	(wore)	bore	fore
8	care	(care)	Clare	dare	rare

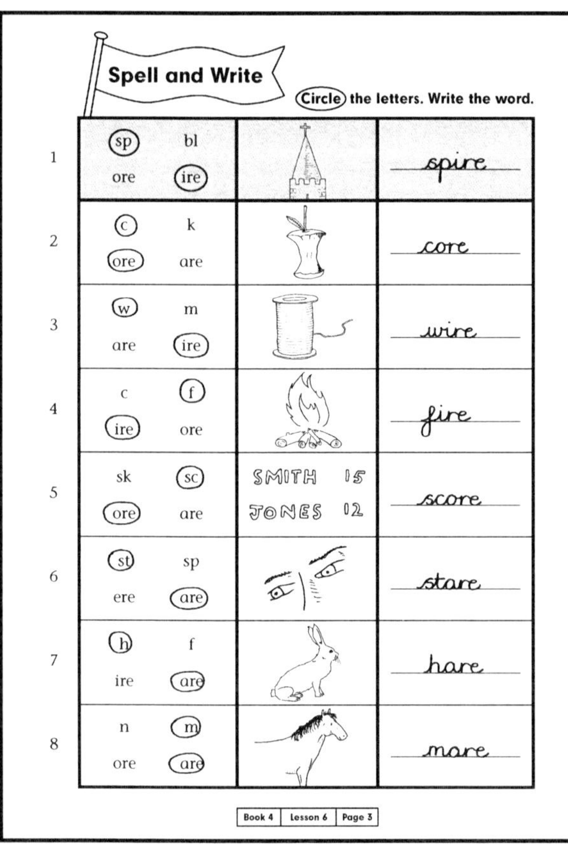

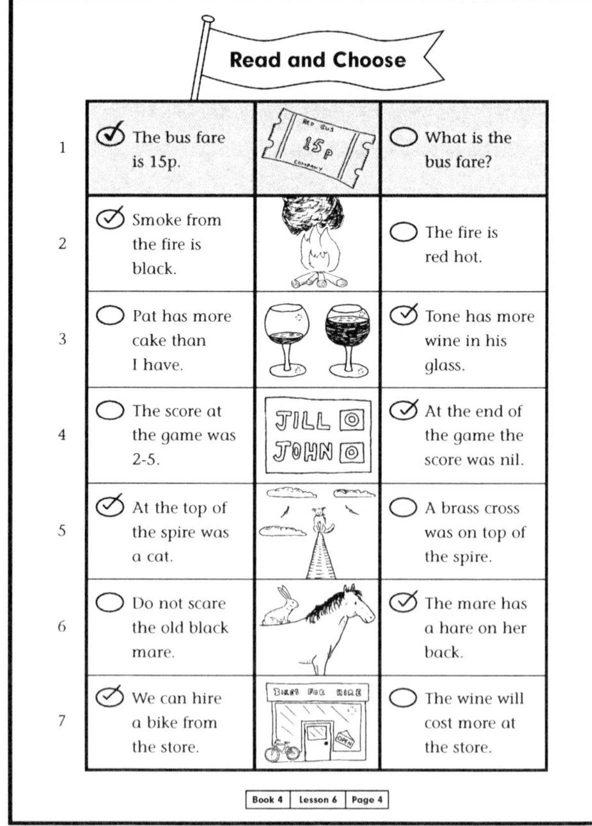

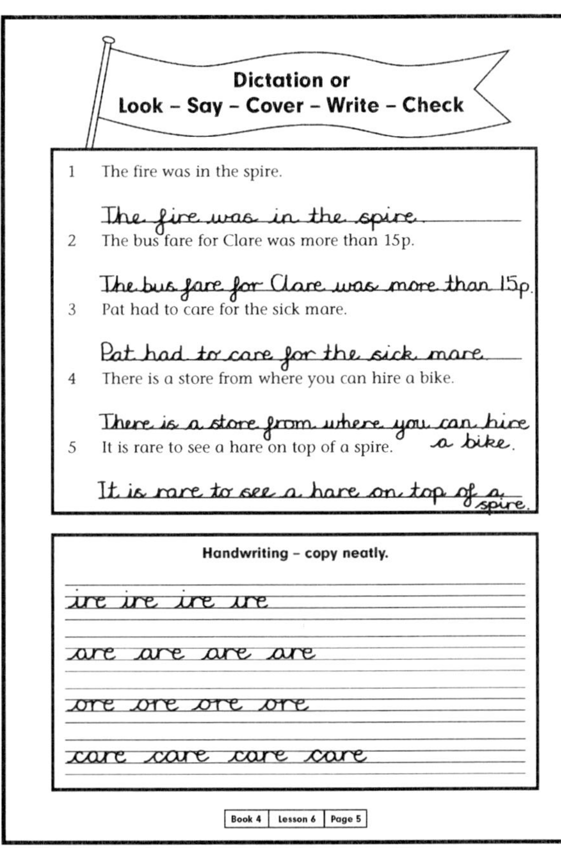

1 The fire was in the spire.

The fire was in the spire.

2 The bus fare for Clare was more than 15p.

The bus fare for Clare was more than 15p.

3 Pat had to care for the sick mare.

Pat had to care for the sick mare.

4 There is a store from where you can hire a bike.

There is a store from where you can hire a bike.

5 It is rare to see a hare on top of a spire.

It is rare to see a hare on top of a spire.

Handwriting – copy neatly.

ire ire ire ire

are are are are

ore ore ore ore

care care care care

Book 4 | Lesson 6 | Page 5

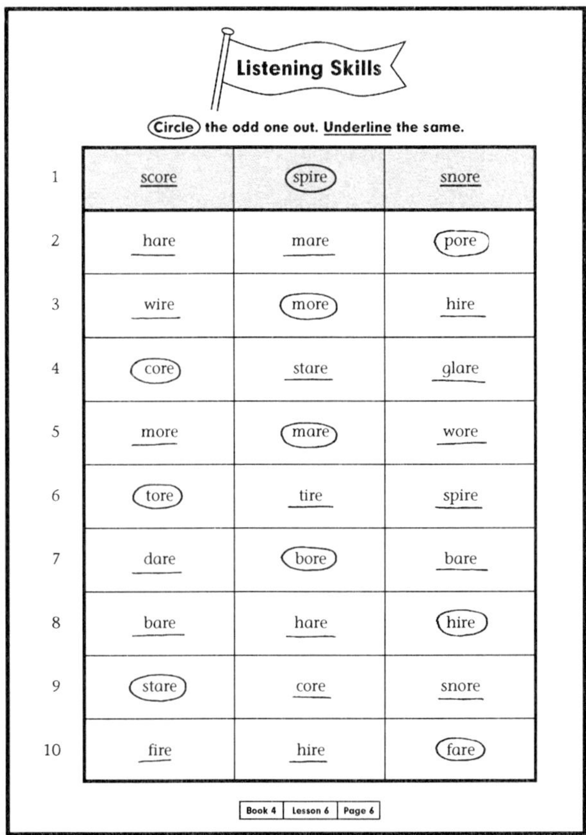

Circle the odd one out. Underline the same.

1	score	(spire)	snore
2	hare	mare	(pore)
3	wire	(more)	hire
4	(core)	stare	glare
5	more	(mare)	wore
6	(tore)	tire	spire
7	dare	(bore)	bare
8	bare	hare	(hire)
9	(stare)	core	snore
10	fire	hire	(fare)

Book 4 | Lesson 6 | Page 6

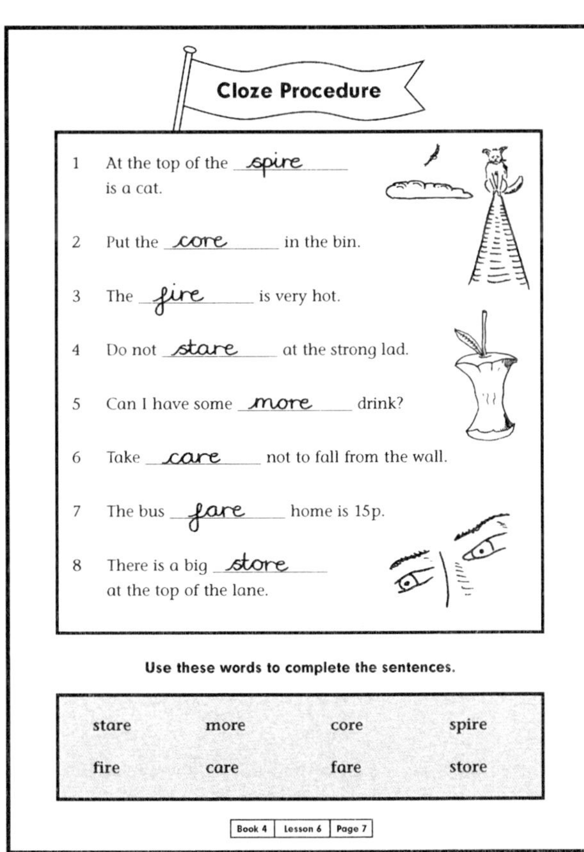

1 At the top of the *spire* is a cat.

2 Put the *core* in the bin.

3 The *fire* is very hot.

4 Do not *stare* at the strong lad.

5 Can I have some *more* drink?

6 Take *care* not to fall from the wall.

7 The bus *fare* home is 15p.

8 There is a big *store* at the top of the lane.

Use these words to complete the sentences.

stare	more	core	spire
fire	care	fare	store

Book 4 | Lesson 6 | Page 7

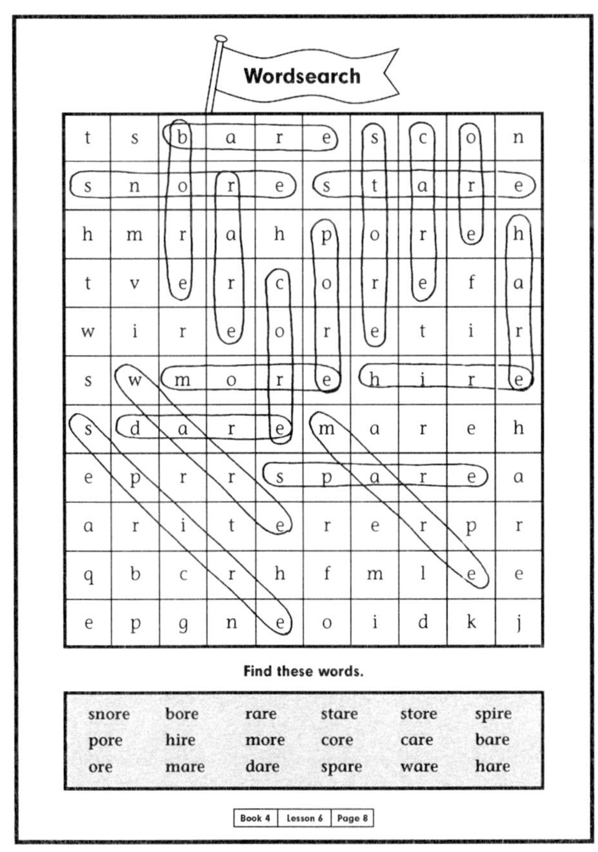

t	s	b	a	r	e	s	c	o	n
s	n	o	r	e	s	t	a	r	e
h	m	r	a	h	p	o	r	e	h
t	v	e	r	c	o	r	e	f	a
w	i	r	e	o	r	e	t	i	r
s	w	m	o	r	e	h	i	r	e
s	d	a	r	e	m	a	r	e	h
e	p	r	r	s	p	a	r	e	a
a	r	i	t	e	r	e	r	p	r
q	b	c	r	h	f	m	l	e	e
e	p	g	n	e	o	i	d	k	j

Find these words.

snore	bore	rare	stare	store	spire
pore	hire	more	core	care	bare
ore	mare	dare	spare	ware	hare

Book 4 | Lesson 6 | Page 8

103

Answers to Lesson 7

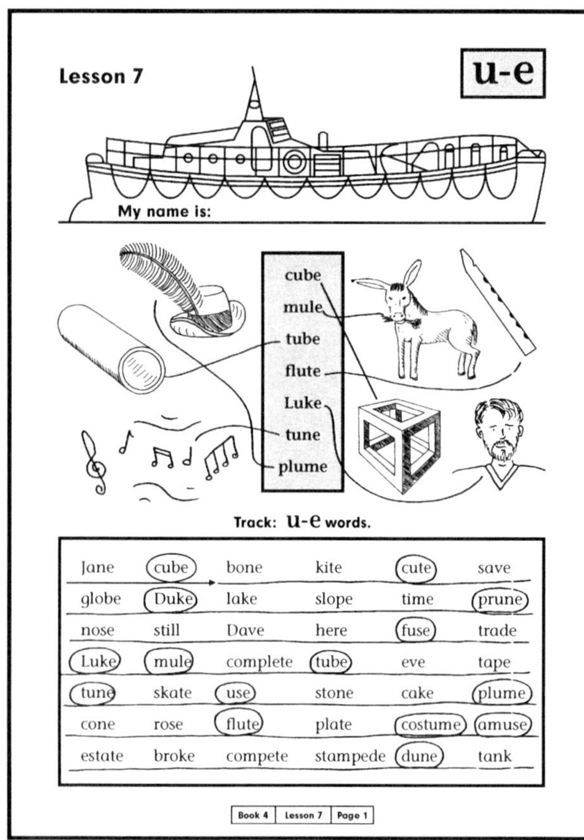

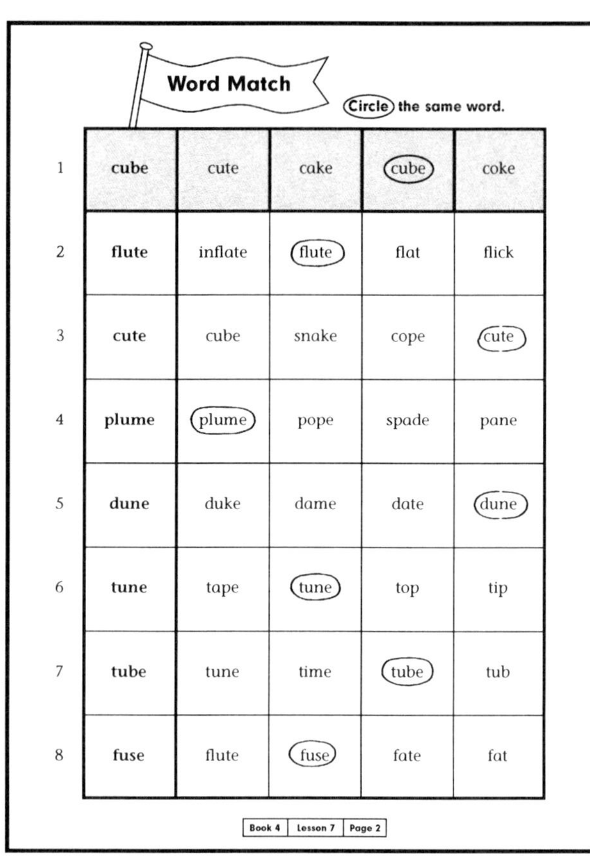

1	**cube**	cute	cake	(cube)	coke
2	**flute**	inflate	(flute)	flat	flick
3	**cute**	cube	snake	cope	(cute)
4	**plume**	(plume)	pope	spade	pane
5	**dune**	duke	dame	date	(dune)
6	**tune**	tape	(tune)	top	tip
7	**tube**	tune	time	(tube)	tub
8	**fuse**	flute	(fuse)	fate	fat

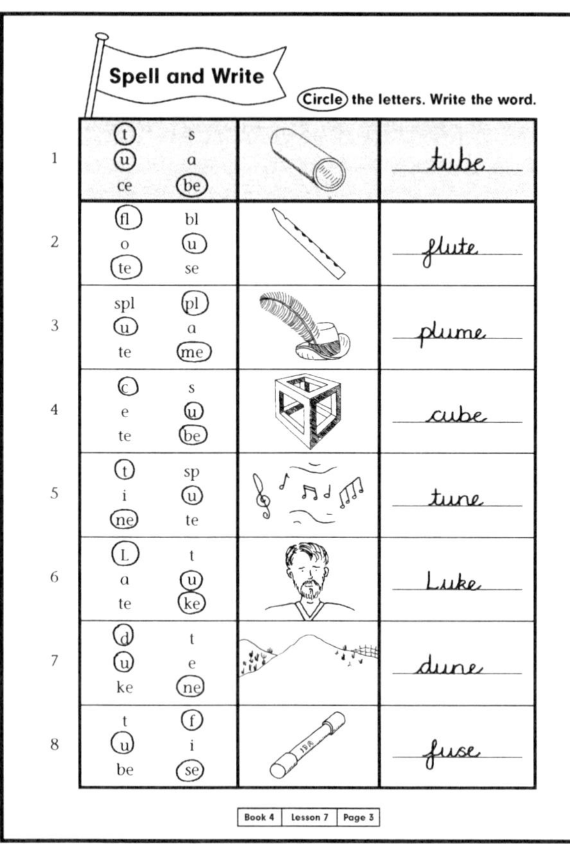

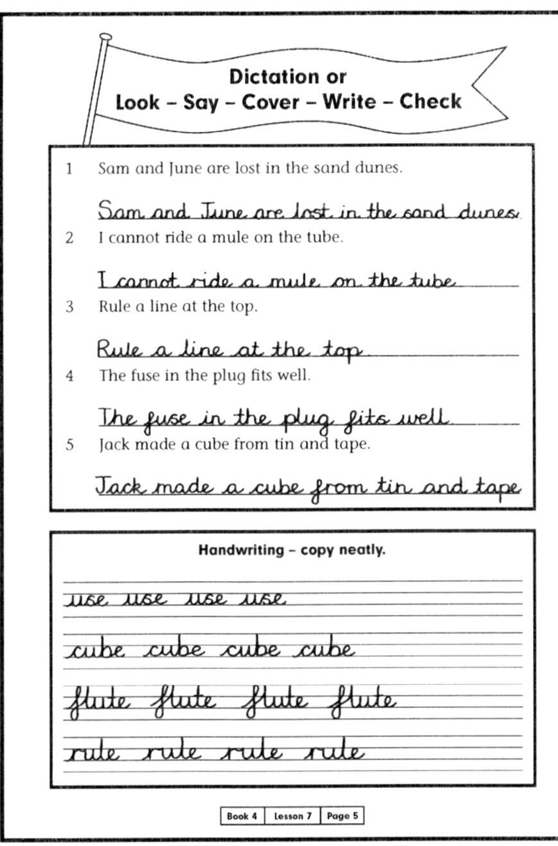

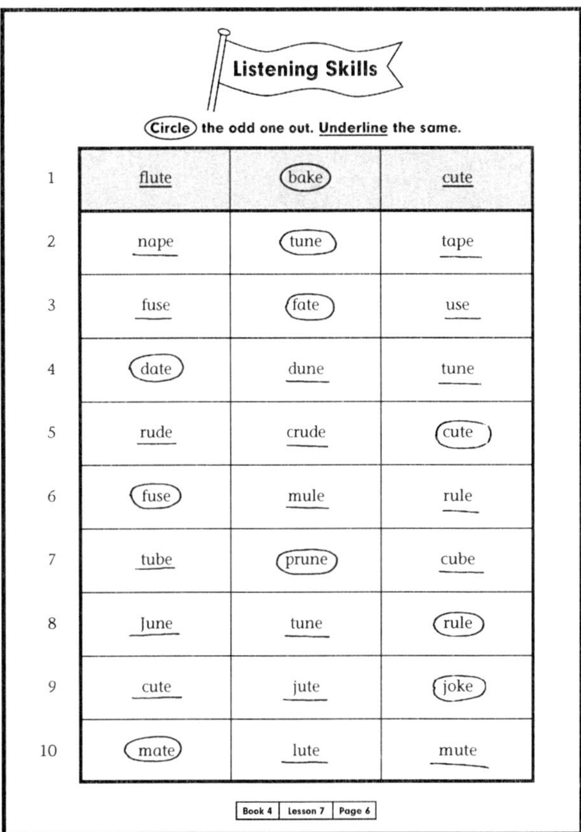

1	flute	bake	cute
2	nape	tune	tape
3	fuse	fate	use
4	date	dune	tune
5	rude	crude	cute
6	fuse	mule	rule
7	tube	prune	cube
8	June	tune	rule
9	cute	jute	joke
10	mate	lute	mute

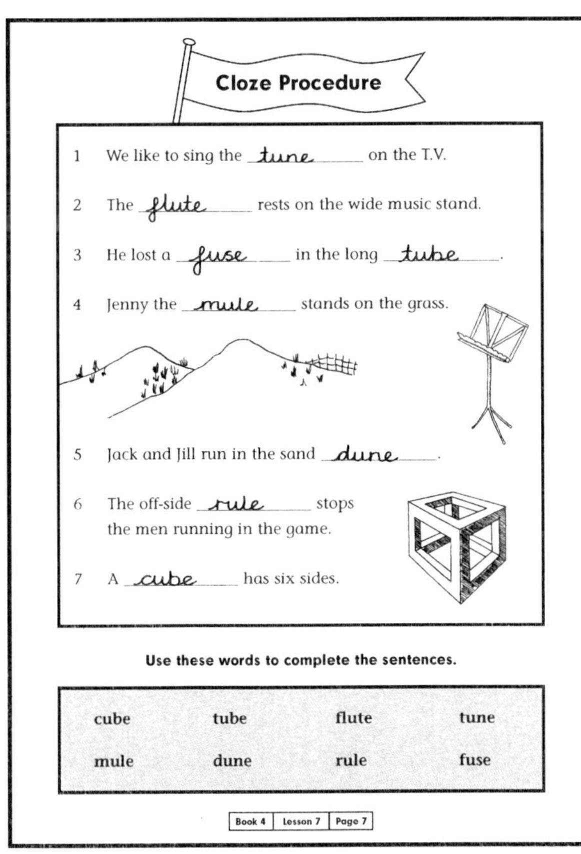

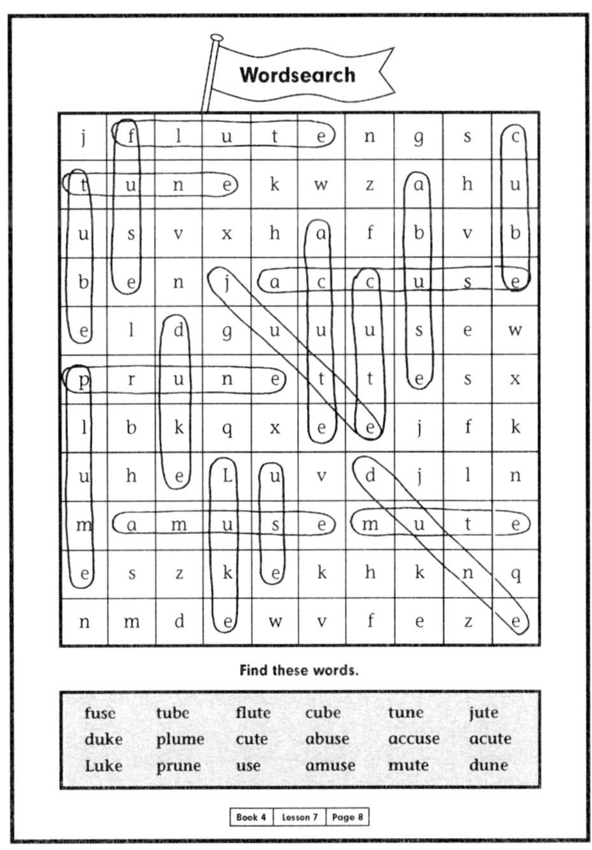

j	f	l	u	t	e	n	g	s	c
t	u	n	e	k	w	z	a	h	u
u	s	v	x	h	a	f	b	v	b
b	e	n	j	a	c	c	u	s	e
e	l	d	g	u	u	u	s	e	w
p	r	u	n	e	t	t	e	s	x
l	b	k	q	x	e	e	j	f	k
u	h	e	L	u	v	d	j	l	n
m	a	m	u	s	e	m	u	t	e
e	s	z	k	e	k	h	k	n	q
n	m	d	e	w	v	f	e	z	e

Answers to Lesson 8

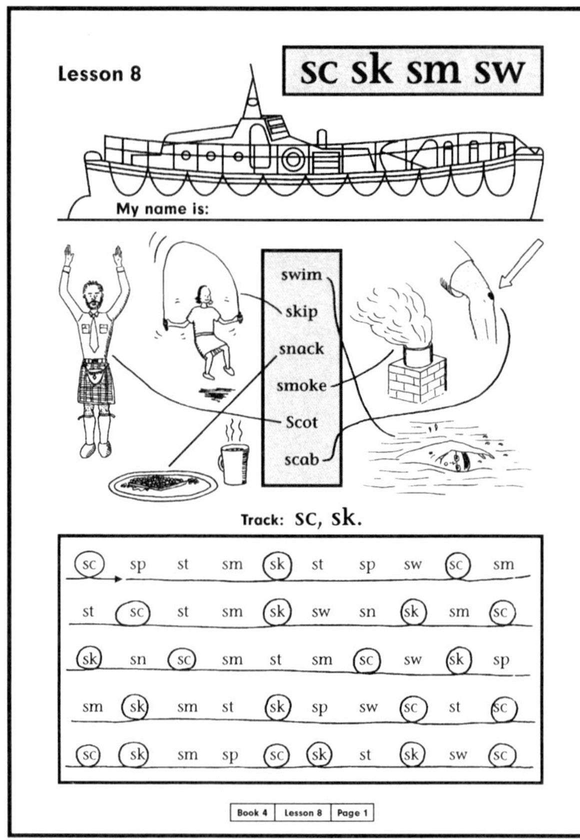

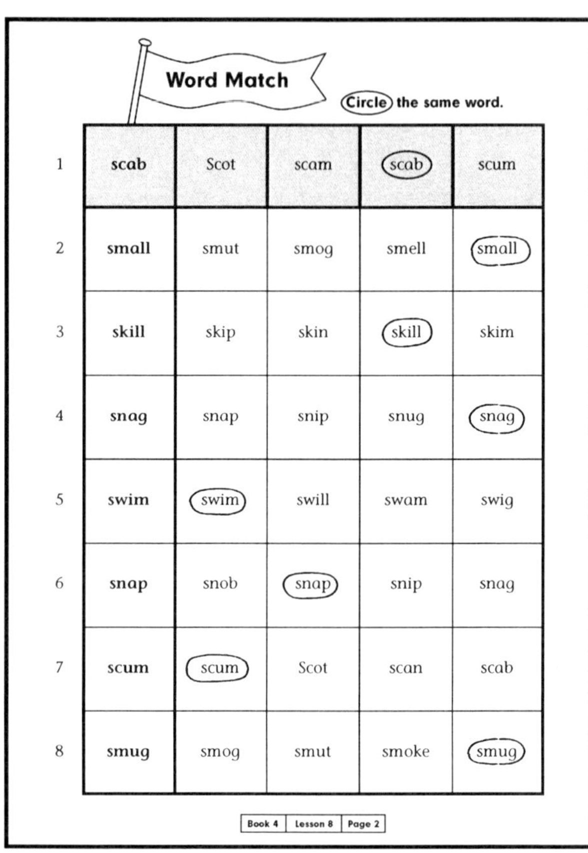

Track box (Page 1):

(sc)→	sp	st	sm	(sk)	st	sp	sw	(sc)	sm
st	(sc)	st	sm	(sk)	sw	sn	(sk)	sm	(sc)
(sk)	sn	(sc)	sm	st	sm	(sc)	sw	(sk)	sp
sm	(sk)	sm	st	(sk)	sp	sw	(sc)	st	(sc)
(sc)	(sk)	sm	sp	(sc)	(sk)	st	(sk)	sw	(sc)

Word Match (Page 2):

1	scab	Scot	scam	(scab)	scum
2	small	smut	smog	smell	(small)
3	skill	skip	skin	(skill)	skim
4	snag	snap	snip	snug	(snag)
5	swim	(swim)	swill	swam	swig
6	snap	snob	(snap)	snip	snag
7	scum	(scum)	Scot	scan	scab
8	smug	smog	smut	smoke	(smug)

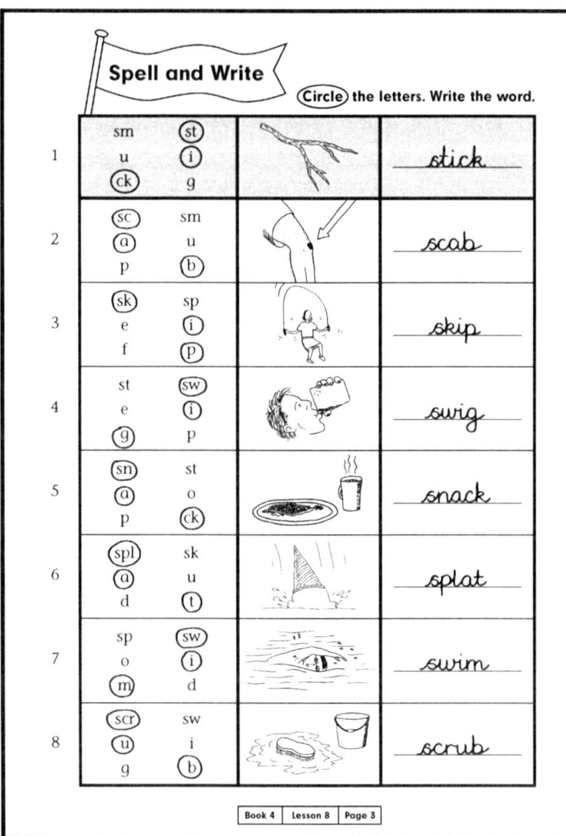

Spell and Write (Page 3):

	letters		word
1	sm / u / (ck) ... (st) / (i) / g		stick
2	(sc) / (a) / p ... sm / u / (b)		scab
3	(sk) / e / f ... sp / (i) / (p)		skip
4	st / e / (g) ... (sw) / (i) / p		swig
5	(sn) / (a) / p ... st / o / (ck)		snack
6	(spl) / (a) / d ... sk / u / (t)		splat
7	sp / o / (m) ... (sw) / (i) / d		swim
8	(scr) / (u) / g ... sw / i / (b)		scrub

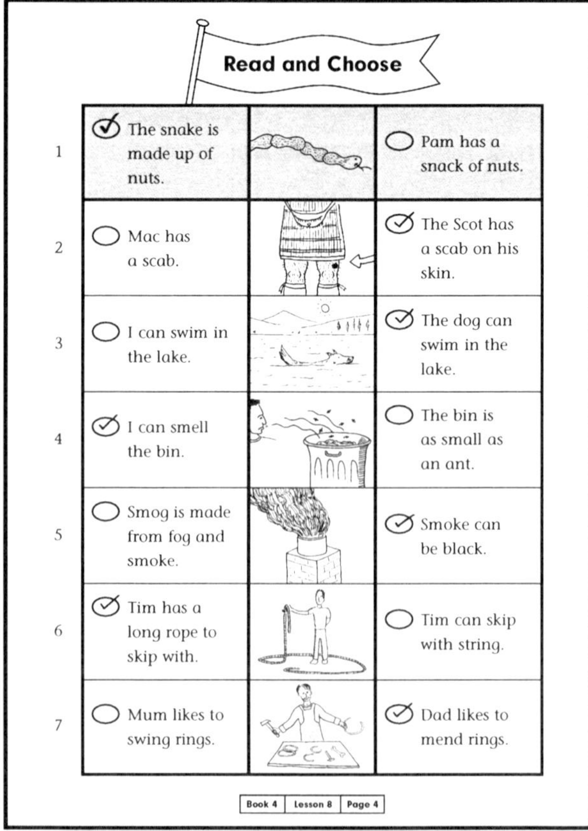

Read and Choose (Page 4):

1	✓ The snake is made up of nuts.		○ Pam has a snack of nuts.
2	○ Mac has a scab.		✓ The Scot has a scab on his skin.
3	○ I can swim in the lake.		✓ The dog can swim in the lake.
4	✓ I can smell the bin.		○ The bin is as small as an ant.
5	○ Smog is made from fog and smoke.		✓ Smoke can be black.
6	✓ Tim has a long rope to skip with.		○ Tim can skip with string.
7	○ Mum likes to swing rings.		✓ Dad likes to mend rings.

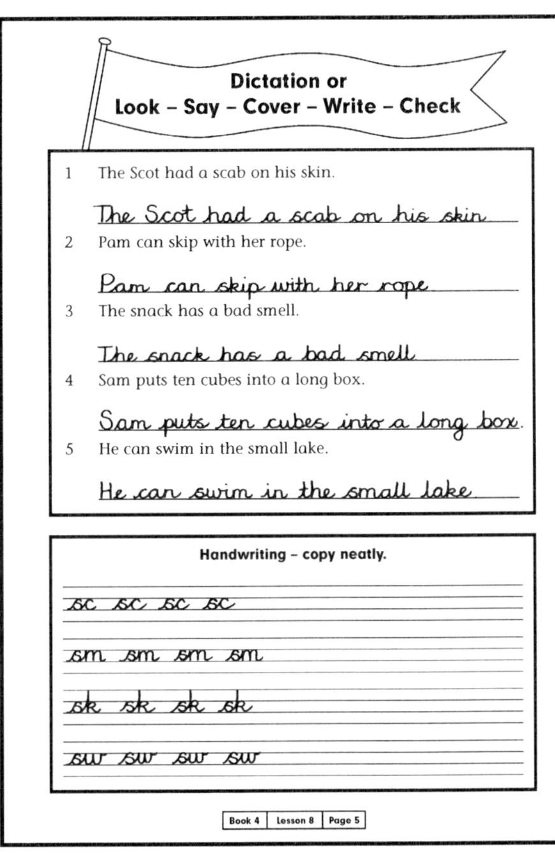

1 The Scot had a scab on his skin.

The Scot had a scab on his skin

2 Pam can skip with her rope.

Pam can skip with her rope

3 The snack has a bad smell.

The snack has a bad smell

4 Sam puts ten cubes into a long box.

Sam puts ten cubes into a long box

5 He can swim in the small lake.

He can swim in the small lake

Handwriting – copy neatly.

sc sc sc sc

sm sm sm sm

sk sk sk sk

sw sw sw sw

Book 4 | Lesson 8 | Page 5

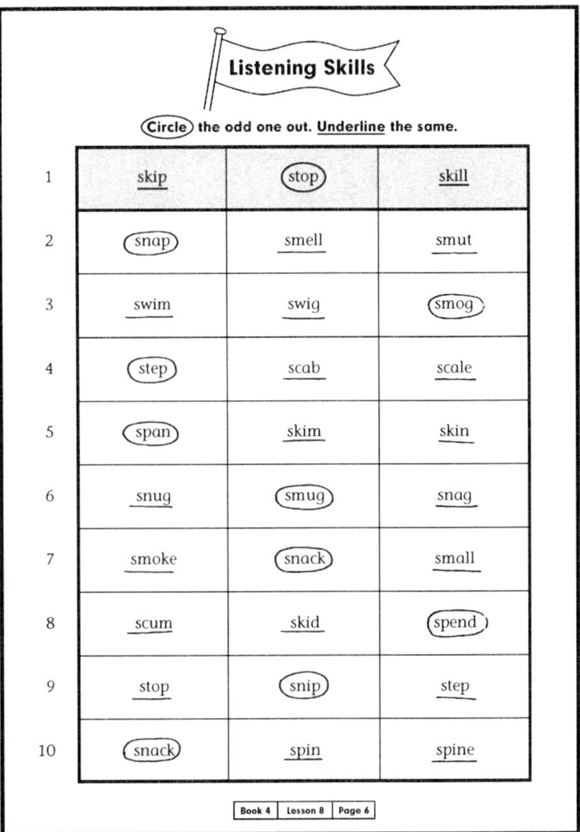

Circle the odd one out. Underline the same.

1	skip	stop	skill
2	snap	smell	smut
3	swim	swig	smog
4	step	scab	scale
5	span	skim	skin
6	snug	smug	snag
7	smoke	snack	small
8	scum	skid	spend
9	stop	snip	step
10	snack	spin	spine

Book 4 | Lesson 8 | Page 6

1 A *Scot* is a man from Scotland.

2 The *smoke* is black.

3 Pam has a rope to *skip* with.

4 The ant is so *small*.

5 *Swig* the drink from the glass.

6 *Smell* the red rose.

7 My *skin* is sore.

8 My mum likes to *smile*.

Use these words to complete the sentences.

small	smoke	skip	Scot
Swig	smile	skin	Smell

Book 4 | Lesson 8 | Page 7

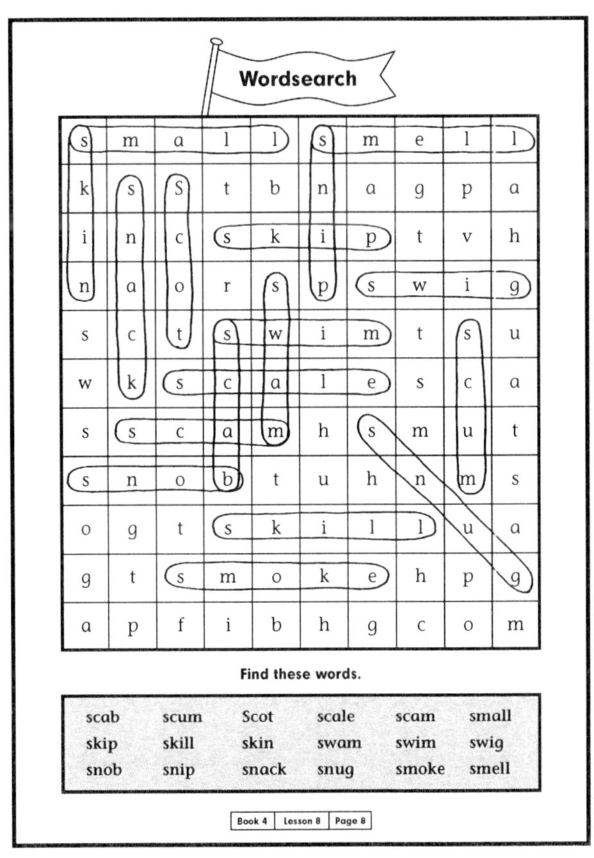

s	m	a	l	l	s	m	e	l	l
k	s	s	t	b	n	a	g	p	a
i	n	c	s	k	i	p	t	v	h
n	a	o	r	s	p	s	w	i	g
s	c	t	s	w	i	m	t	s	u
w	k	s	c	a	l	e	s	c	a
s	s	c	a	m	h	s	m	u	t
s	n	o	b	t	u	h	n	m	s
o	g	t	s	k	i	l	l	u	a
g	t	s	m	o	k	e	h	p	g
a	p	f	i	b	h	g	c	o	m

Find these words.

scab	scum	Scot	scale	scam	small
skip	skill	skin	swam	swim	swig
snob	snip	snack	snug	smoke	smell

Book 4 | Lesson 8 | Page 8

Answers to Lesson 9

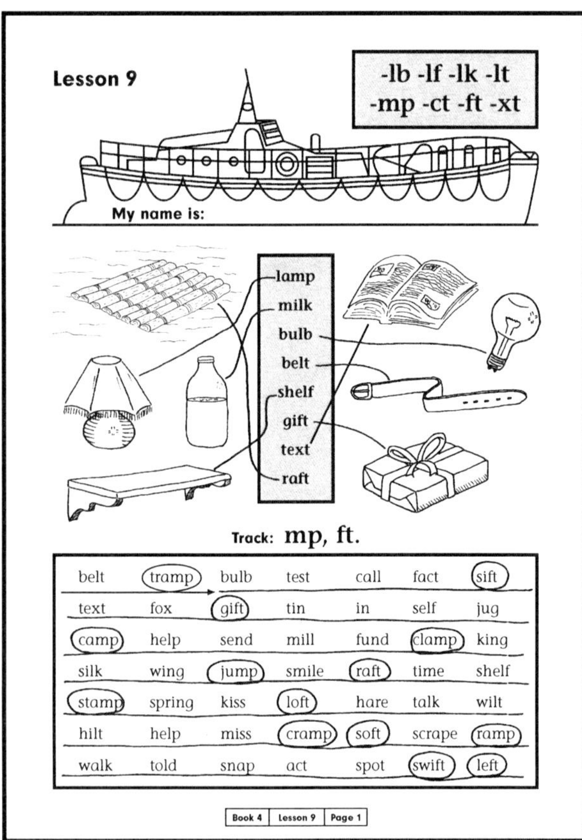

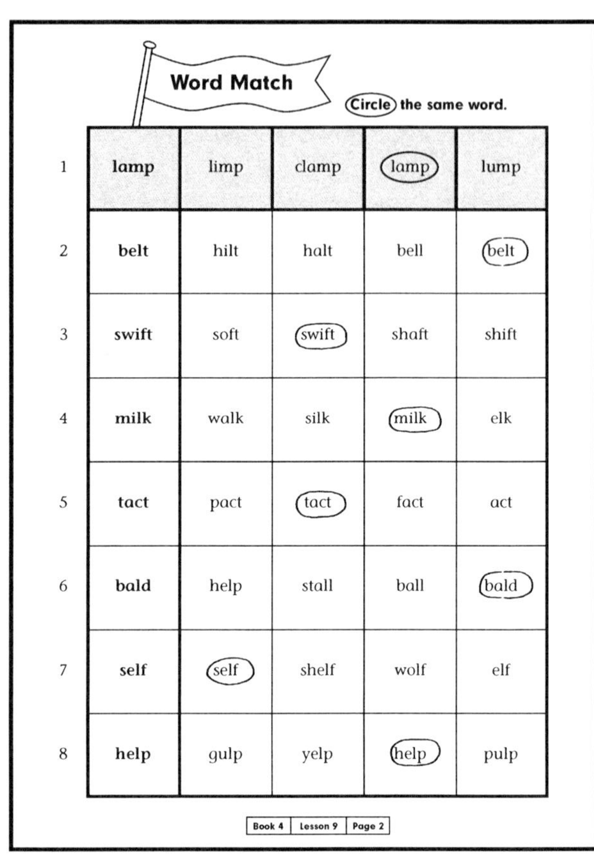

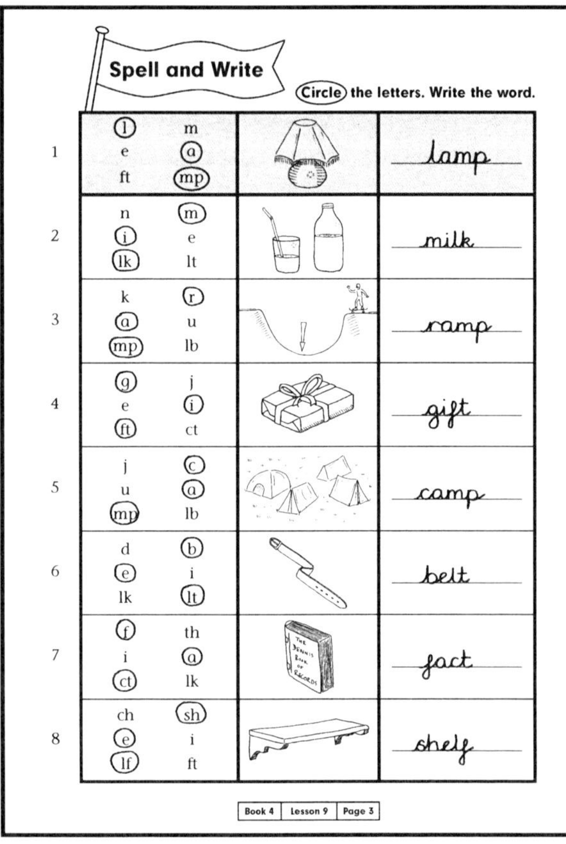

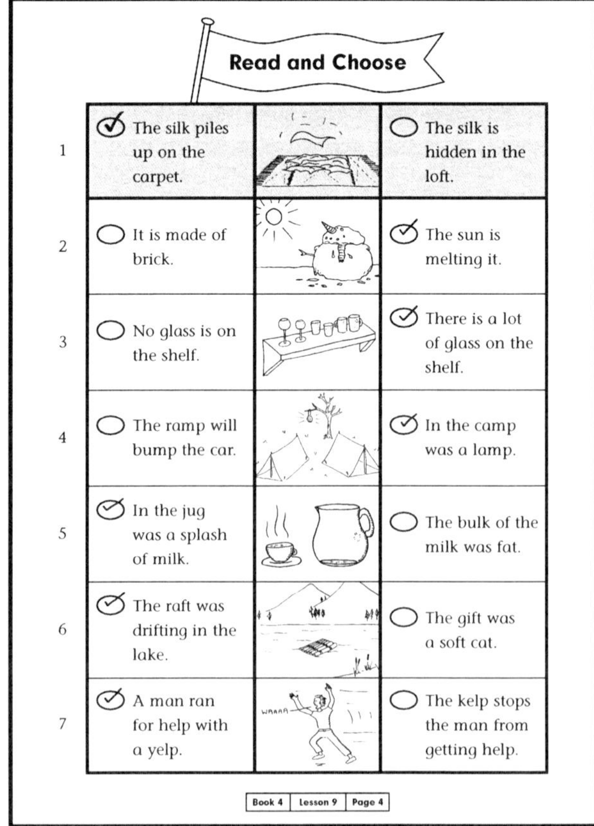

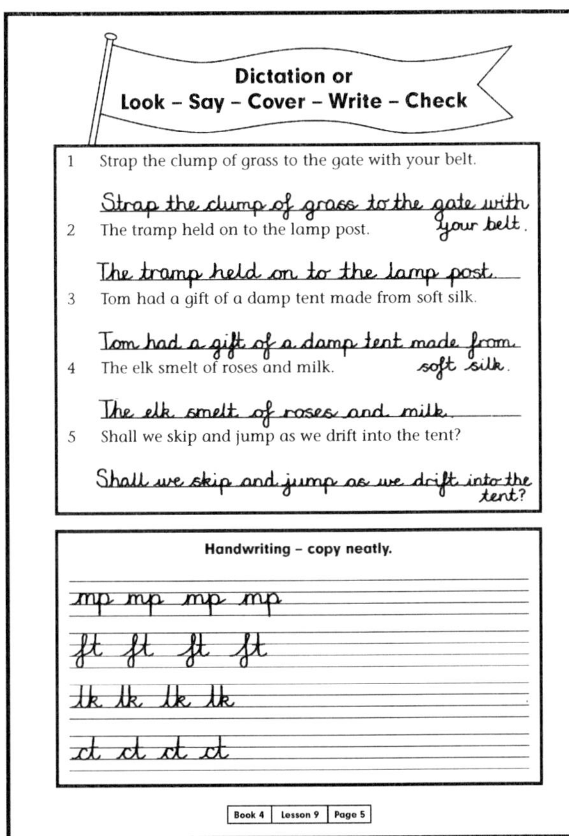

1 Strap the clump of grass to the gate with your belt.

Strap the clump of grass to the gate with your belt.

2 The tramp held on to the lamp post.

The tramp held on to the lamp post.

3 Tom had a gift of a damp tent made from soft silk.

Tom had a gift of a damp tent made from soft silk.

4 The elk smelt of roses and milk.

The elk smelt of roses and milk.

5 Shall we skip and jump as we drift into the tent?

Shall we skip and jump as we drift into the tent?

Handwriting – copy neatly.

mp mp mp mp

ft ft ft ft

lk lk lk lk

ct ct ct ct

Book 4 | Lesson 9 | Page 5

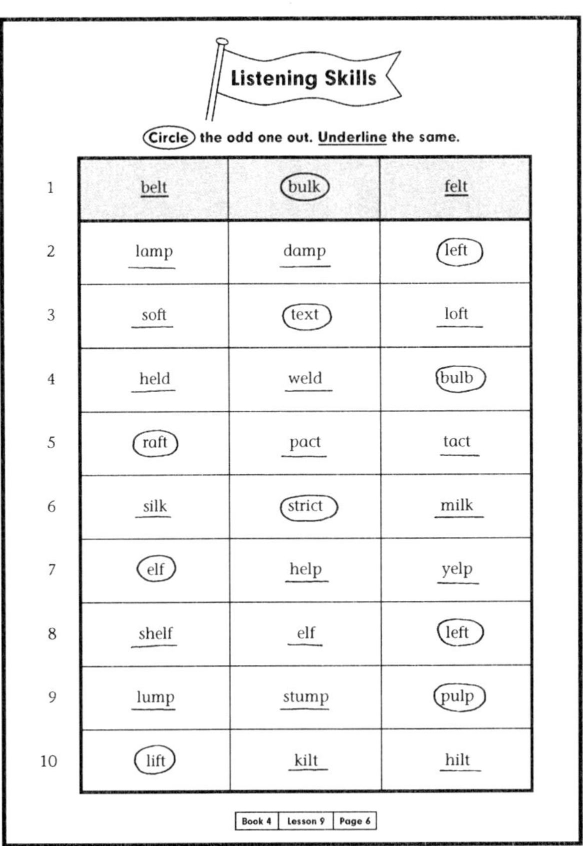

Circle the odd one out. Underline the same.

1	belt	bulk	felt
2	lamp	damp	left
3	soft	text	loft
4	held	weld	bulb
5	raft	pact	tact
6	silk	strict	milk
7	elf	help	yelp
8	shelf	elf	left
9	lump	stump	pulp
10	lift	kilt	hilt

Book 4 | Lesson 9 | Page 6

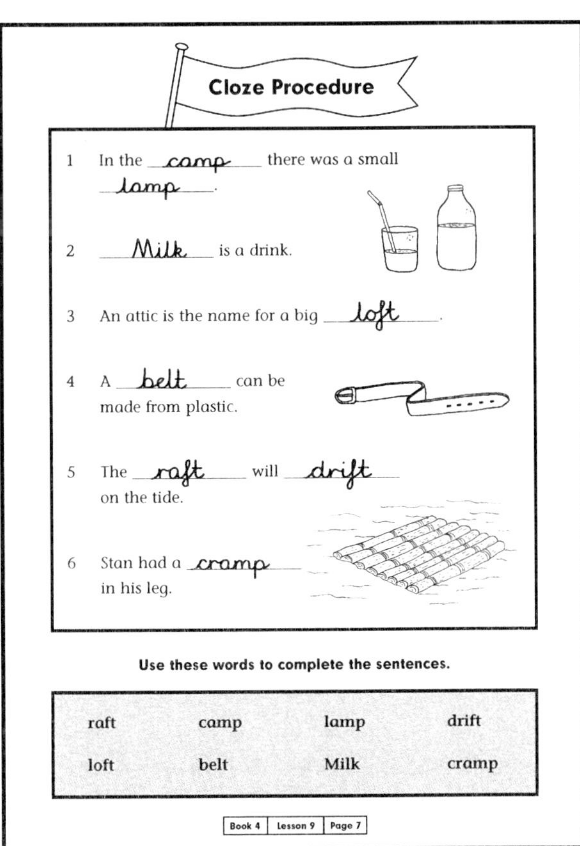

1 In the *camp* there was a small *lamp*.

2 *Milk* is a drink.

3 An attic is the name for a big *loft*.

4 A *belt* can be made from plastic.

5 The *raft* will *drift* on the tide.

6 Stan had a *cramp* in his leg.

Use these words to complete the sentences.

raft	camp	lamp	drift
loft	belt	Milk	cramp

Book 4 | Lesson 9 | Page 7

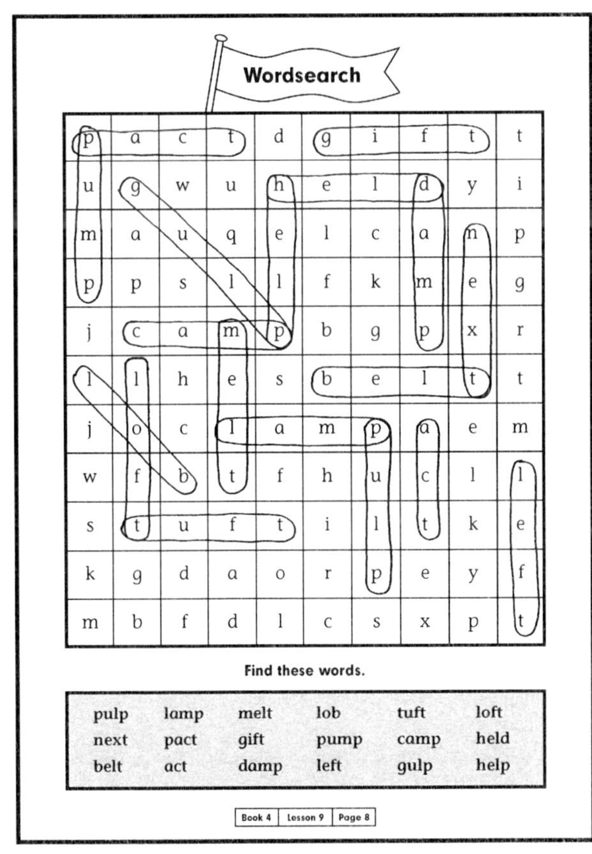

p	a	c	t	d	g	i	f	t	t
u	g	w	u	h	e	l	d	y	i
m	a	u	q	e	l	c	a	m	p
p	p	s	l	l	f	k	m	e	g
j	c	a	m	p	b	g	p	x	r
l	l	h	e	s	b	e	l	t	t
j	o	c	l	a	m	p	a	e	m
w	f	b	t	f	h	u	c	l	l
s	t	u	f	t	i	l	t	k	e
k	g	d	a	o	r	p	e	y	f
m	b	f	d	l	c	s	x	p	t

Find these words.

pulp	lamp	melt	lob	tuft	loft
next	pact	gift	pump	camp	held
belt	act	damp	left	gulp	help

Book 4 | Lesson 9 | Page 8

Answers to Lesson 10

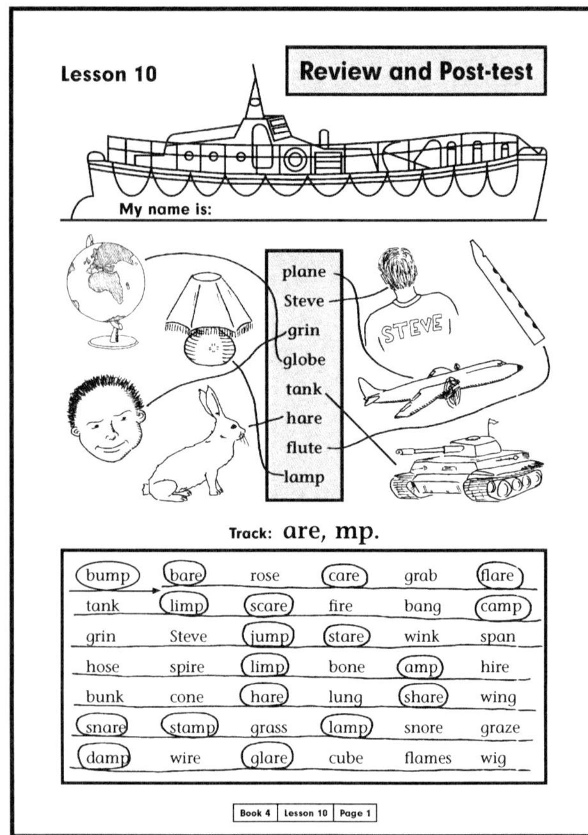

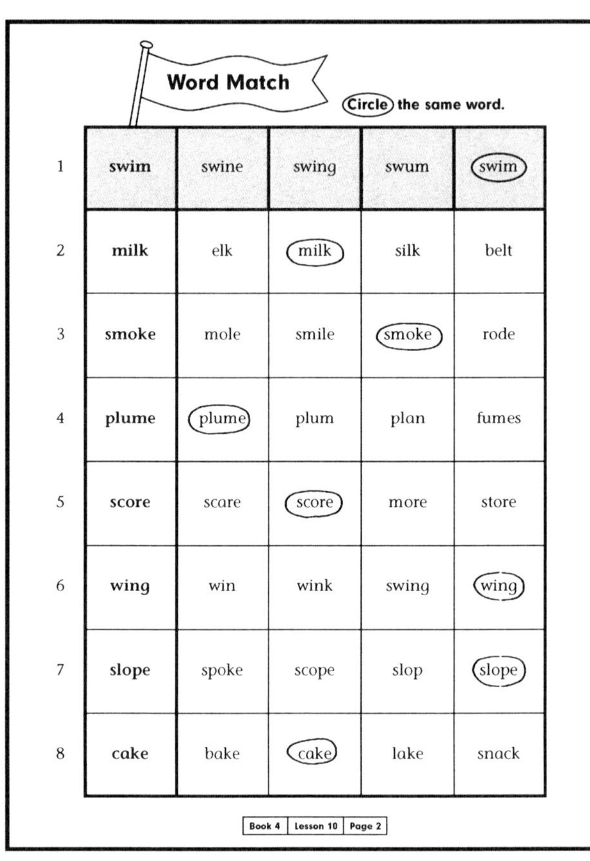

1	**swim**	swine	swing	swum	(swim)
2	**milk**	elk	(milk)	silk	belt
3	**smoke**	mole	smile	(smoke)	rode
4	**plume**	(plume)	plum	plan	fumes
5	**score**	scare	(score)	more	store
6	**wing**	win	wink	swing	(wing)
7	**slope**	spoke	scope	slop	(slope)
8	**cake**	bake	(cake)	lake	snack

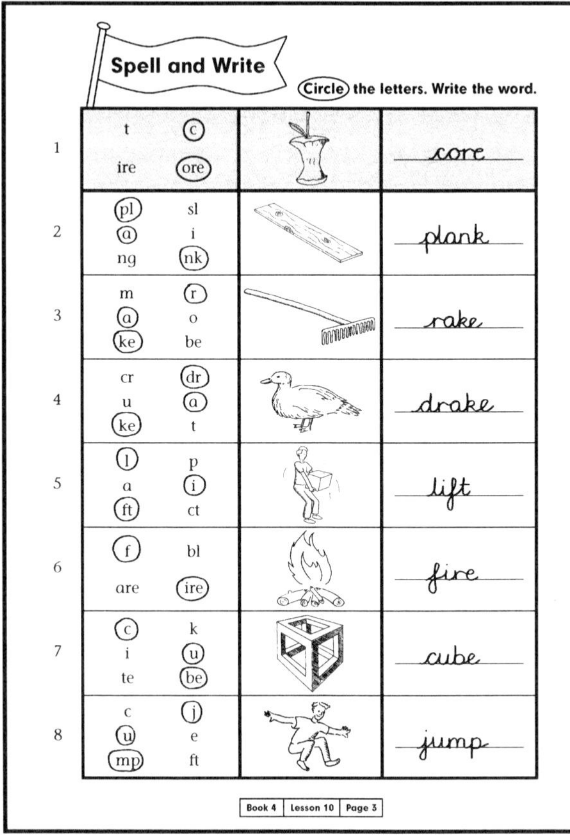

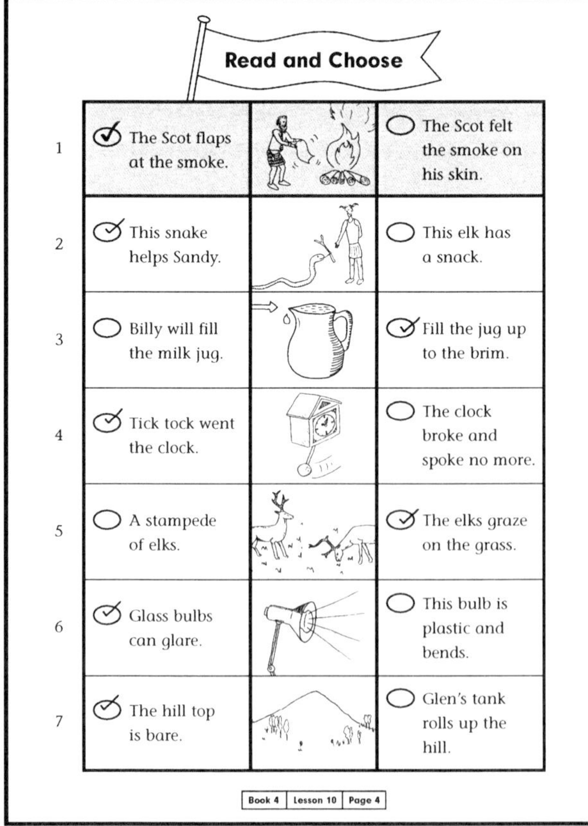

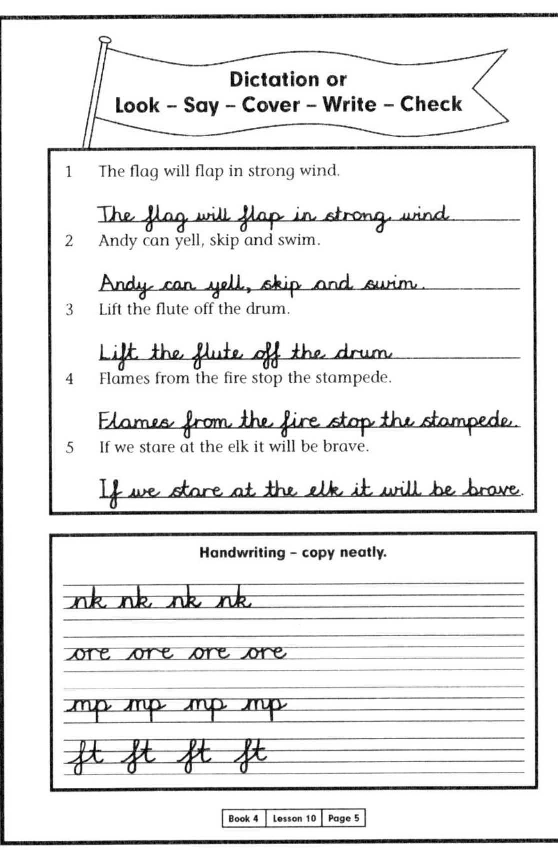

1. The flag will flap in strong wind.

   The flag will flap in strong wind

2. Andy can yell, skip and swim.

   Andy can yell, skip and swim.

3. Lift the flute off the drum.

   Lift the flute off the drum

4. Flames from the fire stop the stampede.

   Flames from the fire stop the stampede.

5. If we stare at the elk it will be brave.

   If we stare at the elk it will be brave.

Handwriting – copy neatly.

nk nk nk nk

ore ore ore ore

mp mp mp mp

ft ft ft ft

Book 4 | Lesson 10 | Page 5

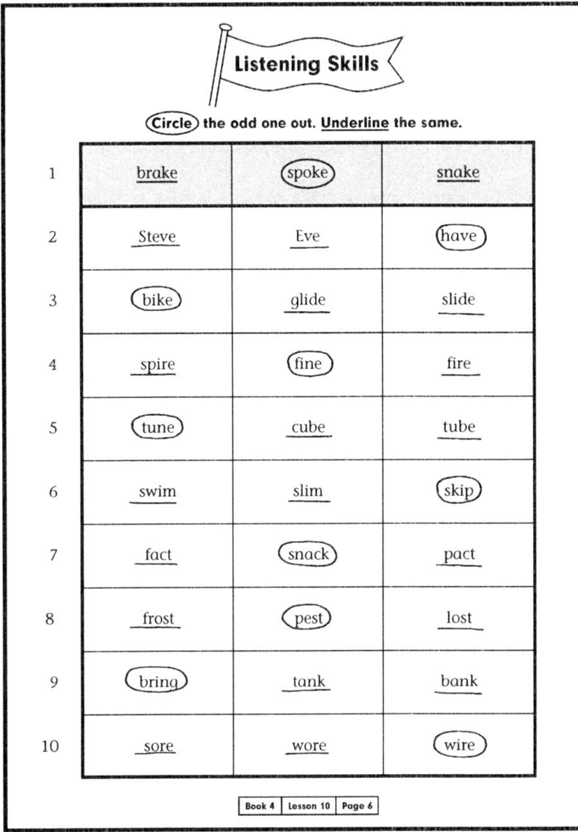

Circle the odd one out. Underline the same.

1	brake	(spoke)	snake
2	Steve	Eve	(have)
3	(bike)	glide	slide
4	spire	(fine)	fire
5	(tune)	cube	tube
6	swim	slim	(skip)
7	fact	(snack)	pact
8	frost	(pest)	lost
9	(bring)	tank	bank
10	sore	wore	(wire)

Book 4 | Lesson 10 | Page 6

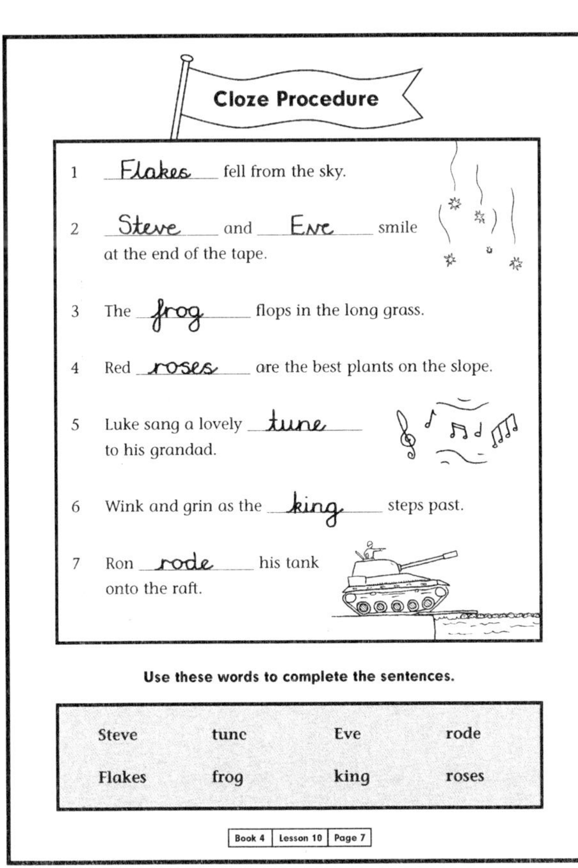

1. *Flakes* fell from the sky.

2. *Steve* and *Eve* smile at the end of the tape.

3. The *frog* flops in the long grass.

4. Red *roses* are the best plants on the slope.

5. Luke sang a lovely *tune* to his grandad.

6. Wink and grin as the *king* steps past.

7. Ron *rode* his tank onto the raft.

Use these words to complete the sentences.

Steve	tune	Eve	rode
Flakes	frog	king	roses

Book 4 | Lesson 10 | Page 7

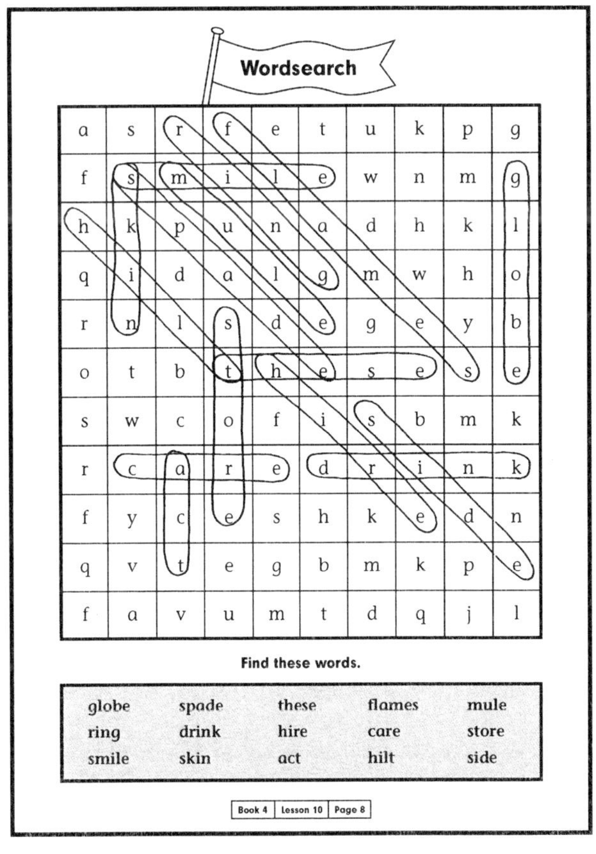

a	s	r	f	e	t	u	k	p	g
f	s	m	i	l	e	w	n	m	g
h	k	p	u	n	a	d	h	k	l
q	i	d	a	l	g	m	w	h	o
r	n	l	s	d	e	g	e	y	b
o	t	b	t	h	e	s	e	s	e
s	w	c	o	f	j	s	b	m	k
r	c	a	r	e	d	r	i	n	k
f	y	c	e	s	h	k	e	d	n
q	v	t	e	g	b	m	k	p	e
f	a	v	u	m	t	d	q	j	l

Find these words.

globe	spade	these	flames	mule
ring	drink	hire	care	store
smile	skin	act	hilt	side

Book 4 | Lesson 10 | Page 8